Also by Calvin Trillin

Remembering Denny

Remembering Denny

by Calvin Trillin

Farrar Straus Giroux

New York

Library of Congress Cataloging-in-Publication Data
Trillin, Calvin.
Remembering Denny / Calvin Trillin.—1st ed.
p. cm.
1. Hansen, Roger D. 2. Social scientists—United States—
Biography. 3. Policy scientists—United States—Biography.
4. International relations specialists—United States—Biography.
5. Yale University—Alumni—Biography. 6. United States—
Civilization—1945– I. Title.
H59.H355T75 1993
300'.92—dc20 92-41932 CIP
[B]

In Memory of William Edgett Smith

Remembering Denny

1

"THE main road leading into Redwood City has a banner hanging over it which reads, 'Climate Best by Government Test,' " the first speaker said. "Apparently, many years ago, there was a nationwide survey to determine where in the United States the sun shone most frequently. Redwood City won. And in the early 1950s the sun shone brilliantly on Denny Hansen. It was a bright and shining moment, illuminated by Denny's stunning completeness. He was a top-ranking student. He was the president of the student body. He was a world-class swimmer and water-polo player. And he was the constant escort of the to-die-for Marilyn Montgomery."

I had been told that there was someone in Washington who had gone through Sequoia High School, in Redwood City, California, a year behind Denny. The other Sequoia graduate turned out to be Peter Krogh, a tall, trim, handsome man—deeply suntanned, although this was the beginning of March. He looked like a diplomat. He is, in fact, the dean of the Edmund A. Walsh School of Foreign Service at Georgetown University. I was surprised to hear him say that the man called Roger D. Hansen on the programs we were holding had been called Denny in high school. I had assumed that Denny was a Yale nickname, adopted to avoid confusion with a football player named Roger Hansen who was a couple of years ahead of us. I wasn't surprised, though, to hear that the sun had shone brilliantly on Roger Dennis Hansen in high school. In the middle fifties, most of the people sent from the public high schools of the provinces to places like Yale seemed to have been high-school heroes of one sort or another. During the 1957 version of Class Day, a ceremony traditionally held the day before commencement at Yale, I delivered what was called the Class History—more serious members of the class presented the Class Oration and the Class Poem and something called the Ivy Ode, which was then done in Latin or Ancient Greek and these days tends to be delivered in some language like Latvian or, most recently, Lakota Sioux—and part of what I said about the thousand or so young men of our class who entered Yale in the fall of 1953 was "Everybody who went to prep school had won a letter in something. Everybody who went to high school, and wasn't a chemistry major, had been president of his high school. There were six chemistry majors."

"My fantasy and the fantasy of all of my friends was to be just like Roger Hansen and all that went with it, including Marilyn Montgomery," Peter Krogh went on. "Denny was the most popular student in a school of three thousand. He was the only student every other student knew by face and name. He was to Sequoia High School what Frank Sinatra was to popular music—the best, very likely the best ever."

The speech was short, and I thought it was just about perfect—graceful, evocative, affectionate. Listening to Peter Krogh talk, I could envision Sequoia High School—or Sequoia Union High School, as we always referred to it at Yale, using the alternate name that had been listed in the freshman directory and that somehow made Denny's school seem even deeper in the sticks. Since my visions of high-school life have always been played out on the same set, the Sequoia Union in my mind looked rather like the high school I went to—Southwest High School, in Kansas City, Missouri—except that the solid Midwestern bricks of Southwest had been turned into California pink stucco and the building was ringed with palm trees. I could see Denny as I knew him at Yale—a strapping young man with a flattop crewcut and a gregarious manner and a broad, absolutely dazzling smile.

In the thirty-five years since we left Yale, whenever the conversation has turned to college heroes and I have found myself trying to explain why Denny was emblematic for some of us, I eventually get to the smile. I usually start by saying that we used to have conversations about how he might someday be President.

Yes, of course, these were joking conversations. As I remember them, their main appeal was the opportunity they offered to discuss which classmates would be of absolutely no value in which cabinet posts, and to make fun of Denny for being such an irritatingly perfect product of the United States of America at midcentury. I had been promised an assignment in the Hansen Administration myself: I would be writing the first paragraph or two of his speeches.

"Just the jokes," he would remind me. "The warm-up. Not any of the serious policy stuff."

"Listen," I'd say. "No human being alive is square enough to write your serious policy stuff. You'll have to do that yourself."

Having such conversations even as a joke seems, in retrospect, an activity peculiarly suited to the fifties. There was an assumption that the society was ours to lead and that preparing what amounted to a leadership class made good sense. There was also an assumption that the society was worth leading. When I went back to New Haven in 1970 to write about changes at Yale—1970 was, depending on your point of view, the high point or the low point in undergraduate disaffection and rebelliousness—I asked a group of seniors whether they had anyone in their class who was going to be President. After a puzzled silence, one young man said, "President of what?"

In the fifties, the what was assumed. Even when I'm talking to people who were in college in the fifties, though, I've had trouble explaining why we made such an assumption about one person in particular. We were surrounded, after all, by people upon whom the sun had shone pretty steadily since birth.

I mention that he was a varsity swimmer. I mention that he was a member of Phi Beta Kappa. I mention that as a junior he won a prize of singular importance, not bothering to mention that I couldn't remember its name or what it was given for. (It was, I eventually found out, the Francis Gordon Brown Prize, whose citation has the ring of turn-of-the-century Yale: it is awarded to a junior in Yale College who "most closely approaches the standard of good scholarship and manhood set by Francis Gordon Brown, 1901.") I mention that Denny was a Rhodes Scholar—or, as I usually put it, "a Rhodes Scholar, of course." I mention what Peter Krogh called Denny's stunning completeness. He was, for instance, a member of Deke, a fraternity associated with undergraduates whose enthusiasm for robust sport occasionally carried over from football and lacrosse to, say, furniture breaking. But he was also a member of the Elizabethan Club, an organization that serves tea every afternoon and on Fridays permits the assembled inside the walk-in vault for a peek at the Shakespeare Folios. It wasn't simply that he was in Phi Beta Kappa; he didn't *seem* like someone who was in Phi Beta Kappa.

Then I say, "*Life* covered his graduation." That sets them back a bit. I add—unnecessarily, if I'm speaking to anyone who was born before the Second World War—that this was the era when *Life* was a weekly magazine and had the cultural impact of all three television networks rolled into one. Then I add that the photographer was Alfred Eisenstaedt. Sometimes I toss in the fact that there was a follow-up in *Life* while Denny was at Oxford.

It was probably the original *Life* piece that made Denny a symbol of achievement and promise—a flawless version of what was then actually called, although usually ironically and often disparagingly, "the Yale success story." But when I try to describe what was special about him, I go from the *Life* piece to the smile. The smile was one reason he didn't seem like someone in Phi Beta Kappa. It was the smile of a candidate—someone who hired Phi Beta Kappas to do his position papers. The smile was the centerpiece of his breezy California style. The smile was what must have impressed Marilyn Montgomery and the Sequoia students who elected him president of the student body and the alumnus who interviewed him for Yale and the members of the Rhodes selection committee. Partly because of his smile, Denny seemed to be the one person remembered by everyone's parents. My father met him once—they spent some time together during that commencement weekend —and from then on a staple of the catching-up conversations I had whenever I went back to Kansas City was a question about Denny. "What ever happened to that Hansen boy?" my father would say. "That boy had a million-dollar smile."

I may have had a particularly strong vision of the smile in my mind because of the contrast with the picture that was on the stage, behind the speakers. It was a large portrait, resting on an easel. Denny looked older, of course. His hairline had receded a bit, and he no longer had a crewcut. But that was not the big change. For one thing, he looked much thinner than he had been in his twenties. As a young man, he was husky, with a smooth swimmer's body. We sometimes called him Fatback or the Whale. The portrait on stage seemed to be of a runner rather than a swimmer—someone without an ounce of extra fat. The expression was extraordinarily intense. It wasn't simply that he wasn't smiling; he didn't look as if he had any smiles in him. When I walked into the auditorium, I had been stunned by the picture. It was a picture of someone I could have passed on the street without slowing down.

Could it have been that long since Denny and I had seen each other? We had become close friends during our last year at Yale—close in that guarded, bantering way that young men, or at least the young men I knew, affected in the fifties. We lived in the same residential college, in adjoining entries. We were in the same senior society, Scroll and Key—meeting with thirteen other seniors in a windowless building two evenings a week in what was supposedly as intimate a setting as existed at Yale. For a while after Yale, we saw each other fairly often. For some years, we'd get together whenever I was in Washington. I could remember the last time I'd seen Denny. After lunch, we walked up Connecticut Avenue and parted at Dupont Circle. He turned down Massachusetts Avenue toward the Johns Hopkins School of Advanced International Studies, or SAIS, as people in Washington usually call it. It was the building I had come to for his memorial service. Those attending—perhaps a hundred and fifty people—were gathered in a rather unattractive auditorium that had as one of its design elements a display of tiny flags of foreign nations. The stage was bare except for the picture of Denny and a bouquet of flowers and the podium. A quartet from a local conservatory was seated near the stage. As I sat in the auditorium, the picture of walking down Massachusetts Avenue with Denny was absolutely clear in my mind, but I couldn't remember when that last meeting was—sometime in the seventies. We were grownups, of course, set more or less irrevocably on one path or the other. We were no longer talking about his presidency.

2

"HIS years at Yale were unambiguously happy times, and he seemed to personify the mythical Yalies of fiction, the Dink Stovers and the Frank Merriwells," Pudge Henkel was saying to the assembled. "Many of you here today may have only rarely seen the Denny Hansen we knew then—the flattop haircut, twinkling eyes revealing his rambunctious spirit, an infectious smile that ignited a room, an inquisitive, energetic, and imaginative mind, richly good-humored but with a piercing wit that could be unsettling and reveal his occasional prickliness. Agonizing over aches and pains that seemed more imagined than real, braced against New Haven's winters in his trademark blue duffle coat with wood toggles, en route to graduating Phi Beta Kappa and magna cum laude with high honors in his intensive history major, Denny in his public persona was fun-loving and in a way bigger than life. Only in his more private moments did he reveal the sinuous course his life would take. In the security of his room or the more quietly intimate times with friends, Denny's more private personality emerged—occasionally withdrawn, sometimes insecure, seemingly guarding himself against the prying world. His success at Yale happened so effortlessly that he responded with an ingenuous disbelief that he had done so well."

At Yale in the fifties, of course, being guarded about personal revelations wasn't the sort of thing that would make you stand out from the crowd. Still, I thought Pudge had noticed something that was present in Denny even at that age—the occasional snappishness, the guarded response to questions that were too personal. Pudge—Oliver C. Henkel, Jr.—is a partner in a large law firm in Cleveland. He and I had talked on the telephone about which one of us should make the speech about Denny at Yale. My vote went to Pudge. Even though Pudge had been a class behind us, I thought that he had been closer to Denny than I was. I used to joke a lot with Denny. He was a good person to kid—a high compliment in my book. He could be teased about being a rube, about being an all-American boy, about being square, about being, somehow, a hypochondriac brilliantly disguised as a lifeguard. He had a sort of mock severity about him when he was being kidded, not far from a streak of punctiliousness that was already quite serious in college. He would smile—not one of his big political smiles, but a slight, knowing smile, to indicate that he was tolerating this impudence out of magnanimity. When I thought about what I might say at his memorial service, I didn't think I'd be on firm ground once the tales of undergraduate ribbing were over. It may have been that I was too conscious of Denny's having forbidden me anything in a speech beyond those first paragraphs—the warm-up. I didn't want to exceed my assignment.

In letters from Oxford, Pudge was saying, Denny mentioned "with increasing frequency his dissatisfaction with Oxford's gray weather, endless hours of study, cold rooms, bothersome illness and indecision about his career path." I was living in London over the winter of Denny's first year at Oxford, and I had seen him several times. As I remember those days, Pudge's description of what Denny was like at Yale—"Denny combined an open-faced, charming innocence with a sophisticated intellect"—would have still applied. I remember being with him in Paris, where his friends insisted that he had tried to book rooms at the Hôtel de Ville, the city hall, and where I think he really did walk into a bakery and ask for French bread, and where he favored an early precursor of American fast-food restaurants that was called, as I remember, Pam-Pam. I visited him in Oxford, where he complained that the *Life* follow-up piece had presented him as a hapless American klutz who was uncouth enough to ride his bicycle on the sidewalk and who was finding "Oxford's damp chill even more challenging than its curriculum." I remember telling him, as I stood in the garret he occupied in Magdalen, that complaints about that "damp chill" line would be more effective if he delivered them without two blankets wrapped around him. In those days, only a dozen years after the end of the war, England seemed a much more foreign place than it seems now—a place where undergraduates invited each other to tea two weeks in advance by formal note and where people of all kinds spoke of central heating as a frivolous and basically unhealthy affectation favored by Americans.

"A disquieting tension between past and future began

to emerge," Pudge went on. "Denny was not quite sure why so many wonderful things happened to him. Maybe too much happened to Denny too quickly, too many accolades at too young an age. We create enormous expectations for talented people. Do we ask too much of our most able young people? Denny talked often of becoming the governor of California, but that wasn't enough. The memory of Denny is dominated for many of us by the assumption that he would one day be President. It sounds silly and presumptuous, I know, but such was the mark of this young man. What an enormous burden for a young person who may not have had the emotional or social strength to absorb such a claim and not entangle his soul. A fear of failure and disappointing others can be paralyzing, and we can suffocate our young by creating unrealistic expectations. His disappointment over the rejection of his application for the Foreign Service, because of his bad back, after the Woodrow Wilson School, at Princeton, was a failed dream. He seemed to have difficulty picking up his direction after that. The lesson of Denny's young life wrestles in our gut. It came to Denny so naturally, so effortlessly. I wonder if he was prepared for the inevitable reverses. It is difficult enough to fulfill one's own expectations, let alone those of an entire community."

I wanted to say that the part about Denny's becoming President was sort of a joke, but I had to admit that it was a joke we never forgot. At our twenty-fifth Yale reunion, in 1982, Denny didn't appear. "Naturally Hansen can't show his face," I said to some of the people who had been close to him. "He's not the President. Even worse, he's not on track for being President. You don't go from being a professor of international relations to being President." A year or two after the reunion, Pudge Henkel, who had gone to Yale Law School with Gary Hart, became the manager of the Hart presidential campaign. I called a classmate. "Can't you see what's happening?" I said. "Hart becomes the President. He needs a national-security adviser. Whose counsel does he seek in finding someone? Pudge's, of course—his loyal campaign manager. Pudge says, 'I know a smart guy at Johns Hopkins—Roger D. Hansen.' Hansen does very well. Hart self-destructs. Next time around, the Democrats nominate somebody else for President, but they need someone from the 'Hart wing of the party' on the ticket. Who else? Roger D. Hansen. He's elected Vice President. The President dies. Hansen succeeds him. He shows up at the thirty-fifth reunion up to his ass in Secret Service men. He's got that knowing smile on his face all weekend: we were just impatient. Why couldn't we see it at the twenty-fifth?"

After Pudge sat down, there weren't any more references to anyone named Denny. At some point—I remembered it as just after Oxford—Denny had decided that he couldn't go through life with what he considered a kid's nickname, and the SAIS people knew him as Roger Hansen. The expectation that the Roger speeches would bring a change of tone as well as a change of name had been confirmed when the dean of SAIS, George R. Packard, in the course of introducing the program, had reminded us that the person being memorialized was in the last years of his life "not the man we knew in early better years and not the man we shall remember in the future."

Isaiah Frank, a professor of economics at SAIS for many

years, was the first of the Roger speakers. He had the look of a kindly man, and he spoke in a kindly way about Denny. He told of the obvious talents Denny had displayed as a doctoral student, and of his triumph in turning his dissertation, "The Politics of Mexican Development," into a widely acclaimed book, and of the fine work he had done on a White House commission Frank put together in the early seventies to study American trade policies. "But the success of this work did not go to Roger's head," Frank said. "Far from it. He remained modest, and all too often even disparaging of his achievements. I sometimes think that this was at the root of Roger's problems. The esteem in which he was held by others never seemed to be matched by equivalent self-esteem."

Robert Tucker, the next speaker, had himself just retired from SAIS as the Christian A. Herter Professor of American Foreign Policy, and had flown in from Santa Fe for the service. He had been described to me as Denny's mentor at SAIS, but also as a man who had been involved in a terrible row with Denny some months before—a row that had been triggered, I gathered, by Denny's refusal to show a little flexibility about some rules having to do with the defense of a dissertation. In the discussions I had been involved in about who might or might not speak at the service—discussions with Pudge and with Tersh Boasberg, Denny's lawyer, and with a couple of Denny's college roommates—some of the SAIS people had been identified partly by the job in government their colleagues said they really wanted to have instead of their jobs as academics, and Tucker, in what seemed to be a SAIS way of saying that the man was to be taken seriously, had been identified as someone who would have, all in all, preferred being Secretary of State.

"In memorializing the life of a colleague and a friend, we cannot ignore the fact that the circumstances in which Roger Hansen died are particularly solemn," Tucker began. "If death is always an event we find shocking, the act of taking one's life conveys an added measure of dread."

3

I had learned of Denny's suicide as I stood in my kitchen in New York early one morning—a February morning in 1991—glancing at *The New York Times*. On the obituary page, a headline over a three- or four-inch story said, ROGER D. HANSEN, 55, PROFESSOR AND AUTHOR. Denny? I couldn't believe it. My first thought was that there were, as we had always known, other Roger Hansens. But when I started the story, it quickly became obvious that Denny was the Roger Hansen in question:

> Roger D. Hansen, a professor of international relations at Johns Hopkins University's Nitze School of Advanced International Studies in Washington, was found dead Friday at the home of a friend in Rehoboth Beach, Del. He was 55 years old and lived in Washington.
>
> Dr. Hansen took his life by inhaling carbon monoxide from his car, the police in Rehoboth Beach said. Colleagues at Johns Hopkins, where Dr. Hansen had

taught for 15 years, said he had a severe back ailment that had required major operations.

Couldn't believe it? As I read the obituary, it occurred to me—and I suppose this was a further shock—that, not having seen Denny in years, I didn't have enough facts about him to judge his suicide believable or not believable. I had always taken it for granted that he was doing well in his career, even if it was not precisely the career we had in mind for him. I knew he held a chair at SAIS, and I had once seen one of his books mentioned in the *Times* with great respect. Did people commit suicide over bad backs? I assumed there were other factors—what the papers sometimes call personal problems. I had no idea of his mental state. I remembered hearing years before that he had been going through a Freudian analysis: the word was that he wouldn't be able to get a security clearance for the Foreign Service until he finished the analysis and thus satisfied the State Department that he was, as his college friends delicately put it, "not nutty." I remembered hearing during the same period that he had been seeing the same woman for years; in my mind, some closure of one sort or another in that relationship may have also been dependent on somebody's coming up with a "not nutty" verdict on Denny.

In the standard cartoon set in the psychoanalyst's office, the patient is not a swimming champion from California with a crewcut and a dazzling smile. I suspect that Denny's plunge into analysis was a detail I hadn't troubled my father with when he asked what the Hansen boy—the one with the million-dollar smile—was up to. The views on mental health I had acquired growing up in Kansas City did not leave much room for Freud: I had always explained the stability of people from my hometown by recalling a sign on the city limits that said "Psychoanalyst, don't let the sun set on your ass in this town." I'm sure I never discussed the subject with Denny. At the time, I suppose I accepted the fact that he was in analysis as confirmation of some vague realization on our parts that Denny's smile covered something rather complicated. Maybe he wasn't all "open-faced, charming innocence." But suicidal?

In the days that followed the item in the *Times*, there was a lot of phone calling. It soon became apparent that it had been years since any of Denny's Yale friends had spent an evening with him or sat down at a meal with him. Some of the discussion on the phone, of course, was about what had gone wrong. Joe Clayton, one of Denny's Yale roommates, said to me that he sometimes thought that Denny had been pushed too far at Yale—by those who saw his promise, and by himself ("This has to do with honors, expectations, and nonfulfillment"). Several people I spoke to reported mentioning Denny's death to friends or acquaintances and listening in return to a story of some other collegiate superhero who eventually dropped out of sight or ended up filling a sinecure in the company of a sympathetic classmate or is at this moment quietly drinking himself to death in a New Jersey suburb—versions of the football hero in Irwin Shaw's "The Eighty Yard Run" who could never live up to that bright and shining moment.

In his speech, Robert Tucker quoted Hume on suicide, and mentioned the physical pain Denny had to live with because of his back. Then Tucker got to the commemoration of a life that he said had seemed so full of promise:

"A quarter of a century ago, George Liska and I had him as a student. We both recognized at once that this was a person capable of high intellectual achievement. The succeeding years did not see that early expectation disappointed. Roger's record of publication would be the envy of many who could not hope to match it. In the study of political and economic development, his work clearly bore the stamp of a creative mind. And if this intellect did not find comparable expression in the fields of American foreign policy and international politics generally, this was largely because Roger only turned his attention to these mysterious subjects in the several years before his death, when an ever-threatening physical disability was already all too apparent. Even so, he managed to complete an impressive critique of American foreign policy in the 1970s, which remained unpublished at the time of his death, and to begin a study of the deeper meaning of those changes that swept the world at the end of the 1980s.

"It is tempting to say that Roger was always an easy and pleasant colleague to deal with. Those who dealt with him, however, know that such was not the case. Roger could be and often was a prickly and indeed difficult colleague, and never more so than when what he considered to be a matter of principle was at stake. It was his fierce defense of principles of right conduct as he saw them that perhaps more than anything else could make him a difficult colleague. At the same time, this character trait, so increasingly at odds with the contemporary outlook, made him a valued colleague. Although Roger lived and worked almost all of his adult life in Washington, he nevertheless remained curiously immune to its ways. In a town dedicated to the worship and pursuit of power, Roger was remarkably resistant to power's lure. No doubt this was in part a matter of temperament. In part, however, it also reflected that same concern with principle and independence of outlook which marked his behavior as a colleague. Whatever its roots, it was to me an altogether admirable trait." It was obvious that nobody who used the shorthand of identifying SAIS professors by what they really thought they ought to be doing in government instead of what they were doing at SAIS had ever been tempted to identify Denny as someone who thought that what he really ought to be was President.

Tucker was followed by three more Roger speakers. Riordan Roett, a Latin Americanist who had been described to me as someone who wouldn't mind being Ambassador to Brazil, recalled Denny's laughter and the brilliance of *The Politics of Mexican Development*. James Robinson, a doctoral student who had been Denny's research assistant, was obviously greatly moved, and spoke only briefly. Robinson was the final speaker mentioned on the program, but at the last minute another SAIS colleague, Fouad Ajami, had asked to be added to the list of speakers. It has been my experience that almost anyone who asks to speak at a funeral or a memorial service wants to talk about himself. There was a certain amount of that in what Ajami said ("Roger was not as famous as I am, I presume. He was a more honest man . . ."), but there was also a lot of warmth in discussing Denny as a friend and as someone who had an almost Middle Eastern talent for gossip.

After the service we all went across the hall for a reception in the Herter Room—named for Christian A. Herter, the Eisenhower-era Secretary of State who was one of the founders of SAIS. A lot of those present were people I had begun to think of as Roger people, as opposed to Denny people—faculty colleagues, people involved in one part or another of the Washington foreign affairs industry. I got the impression that a lot of the Roger people hadn't known about Denny. I don't mean that they hadn't known about the name. They hadn't had any idea that the middle-aged academic called Roger D. Hansen—someone, I had gathered from the speeches and from the little I had picked up third hand before the memorial service, who was not a source of great good humor among his colleagues—had once been a magnetic, heroic figure called Denny Hansen, the sort of person whose graduation from college is covered by Alfred Eisenstaedt. They must have found the Denny Hansen described by Peter Krogh and Pudge Henkel as much a stranger as I had found the person whose portrait was on the easel.

At the reception, some of the Denny people seemed intent on demonstrating that there really had been a Denny Hansen, someone nothing at all like the man whose picture was on the stage. Peter Krogh had a Sequoia High School yearbook he was showing around. There was one picture in it that he particularly wanted everyone to see. It had apparently been taken during rehearsals for some student production in Denny's senior year. The to-die-for Marilyn Montgomery is sitting on top of an upright piano. Her legs are crossed and one hand is touching the back of her hair, in the pose sometimes associated with starlets of the forties. Denny is standing in front of the piano, with his hands in his pockets, smiling. Looking at the picture almost forty years after it was taken, I found it breathtaking. Of course, I was seeing it within a special context. It was a picture of Denny looking the way I remembered him, after all, and remembering Denny was the reason we were gathered. But I think just about anyone would have been struck by the health and the freshness and the exuberance and the optimism reflected in that picture. And the promise. In the fifties, such teenagers would have assumed that the world about to be faced was essentially okay and essentially unchanging and essentially without serious barriers. A high-school student like Denny Hansen seemed to have about him an aura of promise unlimited. Before the reception ended, I happened to fall into conversation with an SAIS doctoral student named Nancy Mitchell, who was there partly because she was a friend of Jim Robinson, Denny's research assistant. She had been saddened by the talk of Roger Hansen's early glories as Denny. "The way I see promise is that you have a knapsack, and all the time you're growing up they keep stuffing promise into the knapsack," she said. "Pretty soon, it's just too heavy to carry. You have to unpack."

4

TERSH Boasberg had invited people to come to his house, in Cleveland Park, after the SAIS reception. I drove over with friends who had known Denny at Yale. On the way, there was some grumbling about the service. Somebody said that part of what had been said by the SAIS speakers seemed ungracious, particularly the remark about Denny's final book not having found a publisher. Somebody said it wasn't ungracious, it was pissant. It may be that we had, to some extent, reverted to undergraduate rankings. The tone of the conversation in the car may have reflected a couple of sentences that nobody actually uttered: "They didn't understand who they were dealing with! This was Denny Hansen!"

In my experience with funerals and memorial services, there has often been some grumbling in the car afterward. It must be natural for people feeling a loss to fasten on some factual error in a eulogy or some way that the setting or the order of service was inappropriate. Of the fifteen people in our Yale senior society, Denny was the third to die. I remember the grumbling on the ride back to New

York from New Haven after the funeral of Mike Dodge —Marshall J. Dodge III—who was killed in 1982 by a hit-and-run driver while riding his bicycle. Mike had been living in Maine, where he was well known as a Down East humorist who appeared on a series of recordings about "Bert and I" and showed up, dressed in a yellow slicker, at college auditoriums to tell stories of lobstermen and farmers in a Maine accent so broad that it was hard to believe he had developed it before he ever entered the state. Mike was unlike anyone I ever knew. The High Episcopalian service in New Haven didn't leave much room to go into why that was true. There were a couple of terrific talkers sitting on the platform, listed on the program as ministers—among them was A. Bartlett Giamatti, then the president of Yale, a spinner of perfect paragraphs in the air—and I wasn't interested in hearing them read passages from the King James version. I wanted to hear what they had to say about Mike. The priest who ran the service, Robert Bryan, had been the other half of the "Bert and I" team, and in delivering the presiding cleric's eulogy he managed to stretch the form enough to give a flavor of Mike. Otherwise, I remember someone's saying in the car on the way home, "the departed could have been a stockbroker." Even as we grumbled, though, I acknowledged that Mike, who was an eccentric but not a rebel, had a traditionalist side that would have been horrified at anything other than a proper Episcopalian funeral and would have been particularly pleased that the closing hymn of the service could be described in the program as "the traditional last night hymn of St. Paul's School, Concord, New Hampshire." I suppose it was simply more convenient to be angry at the service than at the hit-and-run driver, who had eluded the police and would always elude us.

One of the people in the car on the way to Tersh's was Mary Fine, whose husband, Peter, had been the first in the group to die. He was a pediatrician who began suffering in his late twenties from something called neurofibromatosis—nerve-ending tumors in the head. Eventually, the tumors took his hearing. He learned sign language. He wrote a book for parents of deaf children. He moved from lower Westchester County, where he had been working, to become the medical director of the student health service at Gallaudet College, in Washington, the only American college specifically for the hearing-impaired. He was the first doctor there who was himself deaf, and the sort of doctor he was is indicated by the fact that the infirmary is now named for him. A memorial service for Peter that I went to was carried on with a communications arrangement the opposite of what is normally seen at political conventions: some of the speakers presented their thoughts in sign, and someone at the side of the stage spoke the words. The words were about how much Peter had meant to hearing-impaired people—about his determination, his fierce advocacy of sign language, his dedication to his patients and their cause even when he knew that he himself was doomed. I don't remember grumbling on the way home from that one.

At Tersh's, someone had put a Sequoia High School yearbook and the *Life* piece on the hall table. The piece on Denny's graduation was in an issue of *Life* dated June 24, 1957—an issue with Juan Carlos ("Franco's candidate to be King of Spain") on the cover. In addition to the piece on Juan Carlos, that issue contained a long excerpt from a book by Chiang Kai-shek on the impossibility of co-existing with the Communists. It had picture stories on Prime Minister John Diefenbaker of Canada, and Engine Charlie Wilson of General Motors, and the new Soviet team of Nikolai Bulganin and Nikita Khrushchev. There were also a lot of advertisements for the sort of goods that these days are more likely to be peddled in the Wednesday food section of the local paper—Snow Crop lemonade and Swanson chicken parts and the medicine chest supplies available at the Orange and Blue sale at Rexall. The piece on Denny opened with a short text block—written by Michael Arlen, who, on his final assignment as a young *Life* reporter, had accompanied Eisenstaedt to New Haven. Denny's triumphs were mentioned; his hectic commencement weekend was described. There were pictures of Denny trying on his mortarboard and carrying the class banner in the commencement procession and introducing his parents to his roommates and going through the reception line to meet the president of Yale and dancing with his date at the prom and saying goodbye to his swimming coach and being greeted after the baccalaureate service by Charlie Trippe's mother, identified as "Mrs. Juan Trippe, wife of Pan Am's chairman." The headline was A FAREWELL TO BRIGHT COLLEGE YEARS, and everything that followed made it clear that Yale had been another bright and shining moment for Denny.

When Denny and I were at Yale, one of the adjectives in common use was "shoe"—presumably derived from "white shoe." I still see "white shoe" in print now and then, used to mean patrician or old-money WASP: the

Times has referred to, say, Morgan Stanley as a white-shoe investment-banking firm. "Shoe" meant more to us than "white shoe." It could indeed indicate a background of boarding schools and trust funds—something like what "preppy" came to mean a decade later, although without the scorn that term carried with it. It could mean dress or behavior that reflected such a background, even if the person involved came from entirely different circumstances. It could also mean something approaching cool or suave. The varieties of usage were brought back to me when I managed to put my hands on a copy of a little pamphlet called "Inside Eli," which was published anonymously during our senior year. (Its authors were David Calleo, who became a professor at SAIS, and Henry S. F. Cooper, who became a *New Yorker* staff writer.) Written in a tone that may have reflected some exposure to the works of Evelyn Waugh, "Inside Eli" consisted entirely of thumbnail sketches of Yale organizations and extracurricular activities and sports, some of which could be brushed off in a sentence ("No gentleman has ever been known to play basketball"). It said of crew, "A dull, unimaginative sport suitable for the very shoe. Dust off your genealogy, if you have one." It also said, in the course of discussing Skull and Bones, the oldest senior society, "In certain quarters it is no longer shoe to belong to Skull and Bones, especially if your father was a member." After describing the Fence Club, a fraternity whose Greek-letter name most people had long ago forgotten, as "the most pretentiously snobbish organization at Yale," it said of another fraternity, "Zeta Psi tries to be equally shoe."

I've been told that a few years before we arrived the term

"white shoe," which we didn't use, was often heard at Yale, along with "brown shoe" and "black shoe." The white shoe people were, of course, shoe. Apparently, the brown shoe people were the bright student council presidents from white middle-class high schools who had been selected by Yale to be buffed up a bit and sent out into the world, prepared to prove their high-school classmates right in voting them among the most likely to succeed. Black shoe people were beyond the pale. Those six chemistry majors I mentioned at Class Day would have probably been designated black shoe. The fact that the phrase "black shoe" had faded away didn't mean that we had to manage without a term for such people. They were called weenies. I had always assumed that "white shoe" and "brown shoe" and "black shoe" derived from the actual color of the shoes each type was thought to favor—white bucks were still worn by shoe undergraduates when we arrived—but I have also heard the theory that the phrases derived from similar classifications that were used in the Navy during the Second World War to distinguish among ship's officers and naval pilots and those young ensigns and lieutenants who wore their white shoes to the dress-uniform functions that were a regular part of your war if you were attached to the admiral's staff. If the full color-coding of footwear had still been in use when we were at Yale, Denny and I could have both been described easily as brown shoe.

Yale College was then part of the way through a long demographic transition that had begun even before American society was shaken up by the Second World War. It was changing from a place that had been dominated by the sons of the privileged—basically the Eastern privileged—to a place that selected young men (and, eventually, young women) according to some rough yardstick of meritocracy and (again, eventually) some consciousness of the racial composition of the general population. The transition was not totally smooth—as late as the early sixties, for instance, it was revealed that the percentage of Jews in Yale College was not only the lowest in the Ivy League but also suspiciously consistent from year to year—and it was so gradual that measuring the change sometimes required decades. But it was inexorable.

Of course, there had long been a tradition at Yale of the bright, hardworking outsider who emerged as a class leader and may have even saved the Harvard game in the final seconds. The man elected captain of the football team in Owen Johnson's *Stover at Yale* was not Dink Stover, one of the fictional Yale heroes Pudge had referred to at Denny's memorial service, but the greatly respected Tom Regan, who described himself as having "come from nothing." (Stover himself would not have qualified as an outsider by the brown shoe standards of the fifties. His name was already known at Yale when he arrived from Lawrenceville, where he had been captain of the football team and vice president of the school—although he had attained those positions, the reader is told, after having fought his way up from "a ridiculous beginning.") By the time we arrived at Yale, the appearance of the bright outsider was no longer accidental. There was a broad and conscious movement into the white middle class and toward the West, a sort of *apertura* to the yahoos. The alternative to Yale's broadening its base to become a truly national institution was later stated in a blunt piece of hyperbole by Kingman

Brewster, who was the president of Yale during an acceleration of the transition a decade or so after Denny and I had left: "I do not intend to preside over a finishing school on Long Island Sound."

Yale's policy happened to mesh with some plans my father had hatched years before. While he was growing up—in a poor family of Russian-Jewish immigrants in St. Joseph, Missouri, sixty miles or so north of Kansas City —he read *Stover at Yale*. He wasn't able to go to college himself, but even before he married he knew that his son would go to Yale. Although we never discussed the subject directly, I have always assumed that he named me Calvin, which neither he nor my mother could ever bring themselves to call me, because he believed, incorrectly, that it would be an appropriate name for someone at Yale. In the tiny grocery store where he began his business career in Kansas City, he put aside the money that one of the bread companies offered for prominent display and quick payment: it was a fund for Yale. (The bread company would have received its money promptly without any incentives. My father paid his bills on the day he got them; if you had explained some of the advantages of the float to him, I think he might have just shaken his head sadly at the sort of thing some people would do.)

I learned about the bread-company money only after my father died, ten years after he came to New Haven for my graduation. We never had a long heart-to-heart about the Grand Plan that called for me to go to Yale. My father was a shy man, who was particularly uncomfortable talking about personal matters, and to the best of my recollection, we never actually had a long heart-to-heart about

34

anything. As far as I can piece together what he had in mind, though, I think his notion was this: he would send me to Yale, I would have an even start with the sons of the country's most powerful industrialists (*Life* seemed to be reading my father's mind when the only parent other than Denny's and his roommates' named in its piece was Mrs. Trippe), and after that it was up to me. It was a first-generation American dream of surpassing corniness, and I don't think it ever occurred to my father that it might not work out; he had *Stover* as a model the whole time.

Stover at Yale was published in 1911, so when my father read it, maybe ten years later, it was a contemporary account. When I finally read it—not until after Denny died, decades after it had deflected the course of my life—I could imagine my father, living in a house where his conversations with his parents were not even in English, reading, say, the exchange Dink overheard on the train to New Haven, and thinking such conversations were going on at that moment:

"I say, Schley, you were Hotchkiss, weren't you?"
"Eight mortal years."
"Got a good crowd?"
"No wonder-workers, but a couple of good men for the line. What's your Andover crowd like?"
"We had a daisy bunch, but some of the pearls have been side-tracked to Princeton and Harvard."

Reading *Stover* at last, I realized that, however foreign its language, its values coincided with—or maybe helped form—those I associate with my father. Like Dink and his mates, my father had uncompromising notions about upright behavior, and he was honest almost to a fault—or at least to a point of occasional irritation to his family (I might have been the only boy in the history of the Midwest who was not permitted to drive so much as a day before his sixteenth birthday, because driving before you were sixteen was against the law). One of the reasons my father was so taken with Denny when he met him over the commencement weekend was that Denny, who came from a relatively modest background that didn't include college degrees, was a character who had stepped out of *Stover at Yale*—complete with Stover's strict views on honesty and proper behavior, although I have no reason to know that my father sensed that. Denny symbolized, I think, what my father saw as the most important reason for Yale's existence: to turn the likes of us into the likes of them. I don't mean he wanted us to be like them in accent or dress or social connections; he had no interest in that sort of thing. He wanted us to have the same opportunities. That commencement weekend was an important milestone for my father. The first phase of the plan he had started with the bread-company rebate had been successfully completed.

Denny and my father sat next to each other at Class Day. Most of the speakers would have surprised the people Stover overheard on the train talking about their daisy bunches from Hotchkiss and Andover. André Schiffrin, the son of intellectuals who had fled France in 1941, delivered the Class Oration. The Class Poem, "Grass Grows Faster than Laurel," was presented by Michael Cooke, an all-American soccer player from Jamaica who was one of perhaps half a dozen members of our class who could be described as people of color (I'm counting a couple of Asians). Richard Arnold, who gave the Ivy Ode in Latin, had gone to Exeter, but he was from Texarkana—a beginning that prep-school boys might have considered as ridiculous as Stover's but that qualified him in my father's view as a neighbor. Dick read the ode after a characteristically modest introduction, which said, in part, "There is virtually no competition for this post, since the number of undergraduates acquainted with an art so arcane as the composition of Latin poetry has dwindled almost to nothing. With due humility, accordingly, I submit the following lines. I hope they are Latin; honesty compels me to admit that they are not poetry." My Class History, which began "Nothing happened sophomore year," was, it almost goes without saying, sodden with a twenty-one-year-old senior's cheap cynicism. When it was over, Denny told me later with great satisfaction, my father turned to him and said, cheerfully, "If I thought he believed any of that, I'd have him shot."

5

WHEN Denny and I arrived in New Haven, in the fall of 1953, Yale could strike a high-school boy from the provinces as something like a foreign country—a rather intimidating foreign country. Years after this, in reviewing a book by Peter Prescott about his first year at Harvard and recalling a couple of other memoirs published by Ivy League graduates of the mid-fifties, I wrote that "in my official capacity as Corresponding Secretary of the Ivy League Society of Public High School Rubes," I had a question to ask: "If all of these Eastern prep-school types like Prescott and Michael Arlen (who went from St. Paul's School to Harvard in *Exiles*) and John Gregory Dunne (who went from Portsmouth Priory to Princeton in *Vegas*) were not actually as self-assured and sophisticated as they appeared to be, why did they have to wait twenty years to tell us so?" In our entering class at Yale the ratio of private-school graduates to public-school graduates was sixty-one to thirty-nine in favor of private schools. The Eastern boarding-school people had their own way of dressing— what was called the Ivy look did not spread to the rest of the country until a year or two later—and their own way of talking, a drawl through the teeth that provoked me to concoct the theory that the man who had previously made his living stunning the cows at a Kansas City slaughterhouse just before the knife came down had been hired by St. Paul's School to break the jaw of every entering boy, in a courteous and understated way.

Some of the boarding-school people had been to Europe. Some of them had boarding-school reputations as boy leaders that were enough to carry them through Yale. Some of them had taken courses that sounded to someone from public high school like college courses—courses in philosophy, or courses in foreign languages that were neither Spanish nor French. Some of our classmates came from the sort of backgrounds we had simply never contemplated. Although I have told the story for years as a joke, one of my roommates—I call him Thatcher Baxter Hatcher in the joke, since a lot of people in our class seemed to have three last names—actually did tell me that after the war his family no longer dressed for dinner, and I actually did think he meant that they were allowed to come to the table in their undershirts. There were people in our class I came to think of as package people: you could go into a store and find their family names on packages, wrapped around candy bars or flour or beer. One of the roommates Denny was assigned to freshman year was John Mars, whose family produced Mars bars. My boyhood friend from Kansas City who had enrolled in Princeton the same autumn I showed up at Yale—Eddie Williams, whose father was an English teacher at Southwest—had a roommate I never heard him address as anything but Eberhard Faber the

Pencil King, as in "Could you please pass the salt, Eberhard Faber the Pencil King?" There were, of course, at Yale as well as Princeton, boarding-school types you wouldn't joke with the way Eddie Williams could joke with Eb Faber—people who seemed to resent the presence of people they didn't recognize from the cotillion. For them, Eddie used a Princeton phrase that I've mentioned ever since when the subject of evocative epithets comes up: tweedy shitballs.

High-school boys from the provinces may have felt ignorant of some things that the Eastern boarding-school people took for granted—I remember realizing in my sophomore year that I had arrived at Yale never having heard of either Dostoevsky or Greenwich—but most of us, I think, got the feeling that a lot of the rich Eastern people were at Yale because of some entitlement of family or class or money and that we were there because, in ways that were perhaps not immediately apparent, we somehow deserved to be. Many years after I left Yale, I realized that we had been bolstered by a belief that we would have never uttered out loud and may not even have articulated to ourselves: there was widespread circumstantial evidence that, on the whole, we were smarter than they were. Even now, nearly forty years later, I'm reminded regularly that I accepted this proposition as a given: if I meet someone who is easily identifiable as being from what was once called a St. Grottlesex background, my gut expectation—kicking in fast enough to override my beliefs about judging people as individuals, slipping in well below the level of rational thinking—is that he's probably a bit slow.

Still, at first glance, Yale seemed very much *their* place. They set the tone: cool, understated, wearing through at the elbows. Most freshmen everywhere must have moments of feeling alone and far from home, but I doubt if I found that fact of any comfort when I arrived at the New Haven station one rainy day, after having sat up on a train from Kansas City for thirty hours—suffering from some awful flu symptoms brought on by the train air conditioning, lugging a huge trunk, and thinking wistfully of my high-school pals at the University of Missouri sitting down together for a few beers and a few laughs. Remarkably, the entering Class of 1957 at Yale had two people from Southwest High School—a fact of no small comfort, the two of us found, in times of celebration or trouble. Denny was the sole representative of Sequoia Union High School. There were sixty-two from Andover.

I was aware of Denny that first year—I see him in my memory walking across the Old Campus, where all freshmen lived—but I didn't really know him. I remember seeing his picture in the *Yale Daily News* as one of the two people elected as our class's representatives to an advisory group called the Undergraduate Affairs Committee. It was an honor, of sorts, although any truly acclimated Yale undergraduate knew to treat anything that smacked even slightly of student government with some disdain; the *News* story gave precedence to the twelve people elected to the Freshman Prom Committee at the same time. (Serious student government would have required overt campaigning for office—an impossibility in a place where those who wore letter sweaters wore them inside out. Achievement was admired at Yale in the fifties, but you didn't want to be caught trying.) I assumed that Denny's election had been the result of people confusing him with the football-playing Roger Hansen—in later years, naturally, I lost no opportunity to remind him of that possibility—but eventually I learned that, not having become close to his roommates, he spent a lot of time on the Old Campus, where freshmen tossed footballs around or leaned up against the fences to talk about how far behind they were with the reading, and where Denny's smile and his charm and his wit had attracted a small coterie. Much later, I also learned that he had often been homesick that year, as the only representative of Sequoia Union High School, but by the time I got to know him, at the end of junior year, there was no sign of that. By the time I got to know him, he was, well, Denny.

As Denny, he seemed to have a limitless future. We emerged from Yale in June of the year that has since been called a high point in American prosperity. With the peacemaking general in the White House and the Cold War having settled into what seemed to us to be a more or less permanent struggle between the good guys and the bad guys, there were reasons to see limitless futures for a lot of people. When I talked to André Schiffrin after Denny's death, he said the picture that comes into his mind when he thinks about how Yale undergraduates viewed the future in those days is *Stairway to Heaven*—moving up through the clouds on a blissful escalator. We had the usual problems of deciding what we wanted to do, of course, but those problems came partly from the assumption that very little was shut off. As I was reminded by Van Ooms, an economist I met at Tersh's after Denny's memorial service, we were demographically blessed: we were white males who were born in a baby bust during the Depression and came of age at a time when the privileged position of white males was so deeply embedded in the structure of the society that we didn't even think much about it. (In those days, nobody ever asked why my father hadn't put away some of the bread-company rebate for my sister to go to Radcliffe or Wellesley.) People graduating from Yale not many years after us had to face the possibility of not being able to get into a first-rank law school or of going to graduate school and then finding that no tenure-track positions on university faculties existed; people graduating from Yale not many years before us had to face the possibility that they might not survive a war. However much we complained about the draft or about the difficulty of deciding what to do, we were greatly privileged. Under the circumstances, it didn't seem so odd to be talking about what each of us would do in Denny Hansen's cabinet.

6

ALTHOUGH some of the SAIS faculty had been invited
to Tersh's, the people who showed up were mostly
Denny people. There were some Yale classmates. There
were a number of people dating from a period in the sixties
when Denny lived in shared houses in Georgetown in a
group that included a lot of people who had been to Oxford
or Yale or both. There were four or five Rhodes Scholars.
I knew a number of the people present, although I hadn't
seen any of them for a long time. After some wine and
food, Tersh gathered us together in the living room. He
had told me that he was thinking about letting people talk
a bit about Denny, because so many of the people he had
been in touch with had seemed so shaken by Denny's death.
"In some ways, what we have here is not an ordinary death
of an ordinary person," he had said on the telephone.
"What we have is an extremely complicated tragedy." The
living room was large, and there were twenty-five or thirty
people sitting in various parts of it. Most of them were my
contemporaries, although a few of Denny's students were
also there. The woman Denny had gone around with for

a number of years—I'll call her Carol Austin—was there. So was the psychiatrist Denny had been seeing in the three or four years before his death.

By way of introduction, Tersh said he had always been in the habit of drawing up wills for pals. He actually practices historic-preservation law in Washington, but having begun his career working, unhappily, in the probate department of a large firm in San Francisco, he had a certain familiarity with how to prepare for the unthinkable. He had done a will for Denny in 1979. Tersh is someone who has always seemed to thrive on contact with people. He has a wife and four grown children and a vast network of friends; for years, he acted as the organizer and interlocutor and tour director for his Yale class. When he drew up a will for Denny, he said, he had been struck by how alone Denny was—no longer in touch with the family he came from, no family of his own. Tersh hadn't seen much of Denny after that. After Denny's death, though, he talked with a lot of people in the course of making the arrangements that had to be made, and he had come to believe that toward the end Denny had been cut off not only from his family but also from his old friends and his colleagues—from everyone except perhaps his students. With Denny's death, Tersh said, "I think we all feel an enormous sense of closeness and a sense of tragedy of how this possibly could happen." Because of that, he said, he thought it might be a good idea for those who wanted to say something about their relationship to Denny to speak up, in the hope that by doing that "we might get to know Denny, and perhaps each other, a little better."

At Tersh's request, Pudge began. "I was here in Wash-

46

ington in 1983 and 1984, and I talked to Denny on the telephone," he said. "And as was the case with almost everyone here—or everyone I've talked with—he talked on the telephone and it was the same amiability that I recalled, but we would set a date for lunch and he would cancel those lunches. He just didn't want to have lunch with me. He somehow didn't want to bring me or what I symbolized to him back into his life at that point, which was very sad. I fault myself for not rooting him out from his apartment and saying, 'Listen, whatever it is, we're going to talk about it.' "

When Pudge was finished, nobody said anything for a few seconds, and then Joe Clayton, one of Denny's Yale roommates, spoke up. Like Denny and me—and, for that matter, Pudge, a high-school boy from Ohio who happened to have a nickname that made him sound like one of Stover's blocking backs—Joe would have been easily described as brown shoe. He spent most of his childhood in Duncan, Oklahoma; when he arrived in New Haven, he was sometimes called Joe Don. I suppose if people from the Yale administration of that era could be asked what Yale had in mind with its thrust into the country, they might point to someone like Joe. After graduation, he spent a couple of years at Oxford studying history. He's now a partner in a Wall Street law firm, specializing in the financing of huge projects like power plants. A few years ago, his son was the captain of the Yale men's squash team and his daughter was captain of the Yale women's squash team at the same time. "One of the issues I've been thinking about is that in political biography you often see people who have a huge amplitude in their life," Joe said, causing me to remember that at Oxford he had studied Gladstone. "They're up or they're down. They live or thrive on the accolades. And when those disappear the down is very extreme. Denny started that process at Yale College. He was high when he was with people who would feed his myth and his career, and when he was alone or when he was in a private circumstance he was down to the extent of being essentially morose. Terribly insecure. I think it became much more extreme at Oxford, but it was always there. What you may have seen in the last few years to me was the process of playing out the characteristics of all these years. But the public life was huge. Just amazing. To live with him and see these things roll in day after day. Prize after prize. And he never believed it. He never thought he had anything on paper that distinguished him nearly as much as the marks indicated."

I realized that I had never seen that moroseness at Yale. It hadn't been apparent in Keys. Occasionally, Yale senior societies find their way into the news—during the argument throughout 1991, for instance, over whether Skull and Bones would accept women. ("Skull and Bones is like Harkness Tower," the authors of "Inside Eli" wrote, referring to the faux Gothic tower that Frank Lloyd Wright once said he'd sleep in if he lived at Yale, so that he wouldn't have to see it when he got up every morning. "Though it is absurd, we love it.") They're often referred to as secret societies, although they're not nearly as secret as they once were, and the impression is usually given that their members spend hours confessing high-school sins and exchanging early masturbatory fantasies. But the societies in fact evolved from at least two strains. The one Denny and I belonged to, whatever its ritualistic trappings, had grown out of a nineteenth-century literary society tradition rather than those early precursors of group therapy that inspired some of the others. Even in group therapy, Denny wouldn't have been morose: there were fifteen of us, after all, and as Joe said, Denny was always great in a crowd. I did feel a particular closeness to some of the people I had been with in Keys—some of whom were sitting in Tersh's living room. As undergraduates, many of them had been the sort of people whose graduation *Life* might have chosen to cover—team captains or chairmen of organizations or members of the Whiffenpoofs or Phi Beta Kappas or, in a couple of cases, a few of those at once. ("They are the Yale ideal," the "Inside Eli" passage on Scroll and Key said of its members, in a sentence I took to be an unflattering comment on undergraduate standards and values.) But the windowless building—at Yale such buildings are called, I'm afraid, tombs—actually offered a sanctuary from the roles we played in our solemn collegiate pecking orders. I remember Denny as wearing his knowing smile—the one he used when he was being teased—for most of the year. Mike Dodge and I were cast naturally in the roles of people who could never acknowledge to him even the remote possibility of taking him seriously, and as I listened to people talk about him that evening it occurred to me that I had never got out of that role.

Bob Mason was talking about Denny from a couch in front of Tersh's fireplace. Bob is a documentary filmmaker in Washington who was also in the class ahead of us at Yale. "I hadn't thought about Denny in a long time, until I picked up the obituary in the *Times*," Bob said. "What struck me this afternoon is that his story is really not all that unfamiliar. It's really a matter of degree and not a difference in kind, I think. I've come to believe that we live in a time when those people who were golden boys of one kind or another have to take great falls at some point in their lives. And if you don't figure that out in some way and don't find perhaps a different spiritual basis to go on with your life, then it is indeed over, whether it's suicide or drugs or one thing or another." Then Mason said, "You know, the unhappy truth about our time, I think, from the fifties until now, is that you're either a winner or a loser, and that makes most of us suffer a lot."

I suspect he had said what a lot of Denny's contemporaries were thinking—that Denny had been brought down by failure to satisfy what one of our professors always called (quoting William James) "the bitch goddess Success." At Yale in the fifties, there were not only winners and losers but also strong indications that such categories would be an important part of our lives forever. In his speech to the matriculation assembly of our class, in 1953, Richard B. Sewall, an English professor best known at Yale for his popular course on tragedy, referred without enthusiasm to a view of Yale as "a stepping-stone to what we Americans fondly call 'success'—success in general terms, what *Time* magazine had in mind a few months ago when it said, 'As every Yale man knows, Yale is more than a great university; it is also a school for success.'" The greater the success at Yale, of course, the greater the success anticipated in life—which meant that Denny had to lug around a knapsack full of promise heavier than anyone's. A lot of people in the room, I think, would have agreed with Pudge's assumption that Denny avoided him because he reminded Denny of the glorious days at Yale that had not turned out to be an indication of the future.

A couple of other people spoke about losing contact with Denny by means that were remarkably similar—the postponed dinner, the agreement to get together that was never quite taken up, the invitation that drew no response. Carol Austin spoke up to say that we shouldn't take it personally. She said that he had such high standards for himself that he couldn't really be with people unless he could work himself up into "being this sort of superstar," and sometimes, given his moods or his physical ailments, he just wasn't up to it. She talked about a sort of early-warning system on the telephone he had worked out even in the early seventies, with people assigned different codes, presumably according to how urgent Denny thought it was to talk to them: one or two or three rings, then hang up, then dial again. I could actually remember an incident as far back as 1964, when I was in Washington to write speeches for the person I always described afterward as the last successful Democratic peace candidate, Lyndon B. Johnson. I had arranged to have dinner with Denny, and he simply didn't appear. The next day, I finally tracked him down on the telephone, and I said, "You are the only absolutely square person I know who is also unreliable. Most square people at least can be counted on to show up." He did have a pretty good excuse. He had been in a job he hated, something at the NBC bureau in Washington, and on the evening we were supposed to have dinner together he had either been fired or walked out—I was never clear which. I do remember what he told me later about how he came to get the job. Denny said the reason he had been hired was that his boss had read in some business self-improvement book that an executive was someone who had at least four people reporting to him, and this man had only three. So he hired Denny.

7

———

"I would part company with those who said it was the Yale golden boy who had a fall," Rocky Suddarth said, agreeing with someone who had said that there was always "something haunted" about some part of Denny's life. Rocky, who was a year ahead of us in Keys and had overlapped at Oxford with Denny, had been the one who invited Denny to join a group sharing a house in Georgetown. He himself had become an Arabist in the State Department, and had served as Ambassador to Jordan. "I had the feeling that Denny from the beginning was a very troubled guy," Rocky went on, mentioning that he had heard of some "anguish" at Oxford and had been told by Denny that the failure to get into the Foreign Service had been because of the psychoanalysis rather than any physical problem. "I saw him progressively over the years becoming more and more withdrawn, and I also thought he felt that there was something with his mother that had been traumatic that had caused a deep wound in him. So I felt that Denny was the walking wounded from the very beginning.

We all saw the accolades and all that. He was a person capable of tremendous self-discipline. His accomplishments at Yale! He got a First in history at Oxford. A.J.P. Taylor thought he was the greatest. He was capable of incredible intellectual rigor, discipline, and accomplishment. But I never felt that it was the golden boy who suddenly had lost contact with his myth. I had the feeling that what we saw was the unfolding of a very deep psychological problem from his youth which eventually destroyed him."

"I would agree with that very much," somebody said, when Rocky had finished. It was somebody sitting on the other side of the room—an older man whom I didn't recognize. "You people don't know me," he went on. "I'm Ted Geiger. I was Roger's boss for about nine years. Shortly after he came to Washington, he left NBC, or I guess he was fired, and he came to work for me on the National Planning Association. When he first came to work, there was still much of the golden boy—that is, the charm, the pleasure of his company, the wit, the humor, a good deal of gaiety. But it was very evident very soon that there were deep problems . . .

"I had a very difficult relationship with him, a really conflicted relationship. I was the authority figure in his life through a long period, and he had always had difficulty with authority—in taking orders, in doing things someone else's way. I was the object of his anger very, very often. There were long periods in which he couldn't talk to me. We communicated by notes, or through my secretary. We eventually ended up as friends again, and continued to be quite friendly until the early eighties, when, as with all of you, he no longer returned my calls, and finally I gave up, because I could no longer reach him.

"He was one of the most complex people I have ever known. Everything that has been said about his intellectual capabilities, his insight, his originality really doesn't meet what he actually was. I never encountered a mind that had the complexity, the insight into society, history, and foreign policy that Roger had. He could express that in his books, although it was very difficult for him to do that, because he was a perfectionist: he had to research everything. He had to know everything there was about the subject he was writing about before he felt capable of putting pen to paper. When he produced it, it was brilliant. But it was a long, very difficult, and very painful process."

Geiger spoke for a while of the difficulties Denny encountered when he finally did go into government—difficulties that seemed centered on his inability to assert himself within a bureaucracy, even though he knew he was brighter than most of the people he worked with. "But those are just two aspects of a very complex, multifaceted personality," Geiger said. "At the same time, all through those very difficult years of the sixties, the years of his analysis, there were moments when the old Roger would appear—the gaiety, the charm. Somebody said at the memorial service this afternoon how much Roger loved to gossip, and that was perfectly true. He loved to hear comments about his colleagues, about the people he had to work with—to hear somebody say something about them that would put them in their place. I think that was a way in which he could express his resentment at not being able to compete with them in professional situations."

Denny's life, Geiger had concluded, could be seen as an "enormous loss" because he never lived up to his intellectual promise. "That intellectual promise was extraordinary," Geiger said. "He could have *been* another A.J.P. Taylor. He could really have been an intellectual giant had he been able to control the emotional conflict and the inner tension that plagued him increasingly during the sixties and the seventies and I'm sure on into the eighties, leading eventually to the tragedy that happened."

If Joe Clayton and Rocky Suddarth had made me aware of how obtuse I had been not to have understood how troubled Denny was even as a college hero, what Ted Geiger said made me feel that I had known some completely different person. Assuming that Geiger had it right—and it sounded right, partly because Ted Geiger came across as a thoughtful man, partly because what he said had been said within a context of obvious affection and respect for Denny—we had been pretty silly, a few years out of Yale, talking about how Hansen seemed to be making a tactical error by hanging around the East when he should be in California establishing some sort of political base. The person Geiger described not only hadn't been President, he couldn't have been President. How was he supposed to get elected? How was he supposed to get the nomination? He couldn't have worked the room at the testimonial dinner. He couldn't have made the first phone call to the key county leader.

"I hadn't thought of it until tonight," one of the Rhodes Scholars was saying, "but there was another case that was very similar." The person in question had been a couple of years ahead of Denny at Oxford—a Rhodes Scholar named Bob who was an all-American football player, a brilliant student, a proper golden boy. Bob had, in effect, managed to drink himself to death. "The one thing that strikes me about both of these is that I know Bob was extraordinarily ambivalent about his sexual orientation," the speaker said. "I think ultimately that was one of the primary things that brought him to a point where he was unable to deal with his friends. His family broke up. Everything sort of broke apart. And I guess I wondered for some time if Bob—and now, through extension, Roger—if it would have been different if they had been born twenty years later, where I think the question of the sexual orientation of the golden boy was not a sort of primary thing as it was for those of us who grew up in the fifties."

Yes, there was that. Until the day Denny died, it had never occurred to me that he might be gay. If the long relationship with Carol Austin was meant to fool people, it had succeeded in my case. On the other hand, I was remarkably easy to fool. For me, Denny was in a compartment in my mind that had to do with Yale in the fifties, and there simply weren't any gay people in the compartment. That must have been true for most of the people in the room, judging from the remarks that came just after the story of Bob had been told:

"It was inconceivable for us in the fifties. I came out of Yale, and I swore I did not know a homosexual."

"Of course," Carol Austin said, with some irony. "None of us did."

"It was inconceivable that anyone could be successful and athletic and masculine and so forth and be homosexual."

"Probably inconceivable to *him*," one of Denny's Yale friends said.

But, as the phone calls began, in the days following Denny's death, sexual orientation had been one of the subjects that came up. *The Blade*, the gay newspaper of Washington, had carried an obituary of Denny, although there was some puzzlement among his friends and colleagues as to how it got there. Sexual orientation had not been the sort of thing he discussed casually. Some of the older colleagues of Roger Hansen at SAIS had apparently been as surprised to learn about the life alluded to in the *Blade* obituary as they had been to learn about the existence of a magnetic and charming college hero named Denny.

Sexual orientation turned out to be something we didn't discuss much, either. The conversation quickly turned to how frustrating it must have been for Denny not to have a steady production of work that lived up to his potential. Somebody said he was too much of a perfectionist. Somebody asked if everything would have been all right if Denny had produced one monumental piece of scholarship. Somebody said he made a disastrous career move by concentrating for years on what people in foreign affairs sometimes call the North-South Agenda ("a no-win situation . . . a blind alley"). A woman I didn't know said that what had always struck her about Denny was that he made such a strong connection to people but then shut them out. He was so closed to intimate relationships, she said, that for a while she assumed that he was in the CIA.

"He didn't have people he was caring for, and in the same way those of us who cared about him were kept at a distance one way or another," she concluded. "You can deal with all these other things if you have connections with people, which he somehow didn't sustain. And that's why we're really all so mad at him—I'm feeling that now, as well as feeling so sad—because we were here potentially to be connected to him, because we liked him so much and yet he kept us all away at a time when he needed us."

Mad at him? I hadn't thought of that—it was among any number of things I hadn't thought of when it came to Denny—but maybe it was, in fact, fair to describe us as a little mad at him. We couldn't blame this one on a hit-and-run driver, after all, or on a freak disease. Denny had done it himself. I suppose you could also say that he had himself made the decision to be so alone, and it was true that the thought of him in his house by himself—no connection with his family in California, no family of his own, no close friends he was in touch with—made me a little angry. As far as I had been able to gather, practically nobody in the room had seen him for more than a casual hello on the street for nearly a decade, but Denny's friends definitely felt what Tersh had called "an enormous sense of closeness." Most of the people in the room seemed to assume that if Denny had been in deep trouble he should have called them. I had to admit that I felt a little bit that way myself.

Denny's psychiatrist hadn't said anything during the discussion, but after it was over he acknowledged to me that he had been simply astonished to find so many people who felt so strongly connected to Denny. The person he had treated for the past few years had appeared to be completely alone. I suppose Denny would have been astonished, too. I thought of the Dick Diver line that had stuck with me through all of those years since I read *Tender Is the Night* at Yale: "Well, you never knew exactly how much space you occupied in people's lives." Denny obviously occupied much more space than he could have imagined. There we were, analyzing his life with great intensity, I thought, and everybody in the room had to understand, when you looked at it realistically, that we didn't really know him.

8

―――――

THE day after the memorial service, Tersh and I went over to Denny's house—a small townhouse set obliquely on the corner of a pleasant block in Georgetown, not far from Dunbarton Oaks. By chance, I was about to go to California on other business, and I was planning to take some of Denny's personal things to his aunt, Norma Hansen, who lives in Los Gatos, an hour or so south of Sequoia Union High School. The house was gray brick, decorated here and there with the sort of iron grillwork that was sometimes part of renovations done in the fifties and sixties. There was a pleasant brick patio in the back. Jim Robinson had started putting Denny's papers and books in order, but otherwise the house was more or less the way it had been when Denny lived there. The kitchen refrigerator was still decorated with runner's numerals from various ten-kilometer races around Washington—the Georgetown 10K, the Alexandria 10K, the St. Paddy's Day 10K. On each of them, Denny had written his finishing times—all somewhere around forty-eight or forty-nine minutes, credible times for a man in his fifties, even a man who didn't have a bad back.

The personal things weren't terribly personal. There were some studio shots of Denny and his brother, Jerry, as children. There were snapshots of family gatherings in California back yards after Denny was grown, and pictures dating from the part of Denny's childhood that was spent in Hawaii—shots of Denny and Jerry wearing leis, shots of the two boys with their tiny surfboards. There was a picture of the house the Hansens had moved into when they came back from Hawaii, not long before Denny was ready to enter Sequoia High School—a little California bungalow in San Carlos, about halfway between Palo Alto and the San Francisco airport. There were keepsakes like his Yale diploma and his Phi Beta Kappa certificate.

The Phi Beta Kappa certificate was signed by the president of the Alpha chapter of Connecticut, William De-Vane, a courtly and scholarly and much revered man who was dean of Yale College for many years, and by the secretary of the chapter, Hollon Farr, a professor emeritus of German. I remembered interviewing Hollon Farr—he was called Tute Farr—when I was doing an article for the *Yale Daily News* on fraternities. By the time we were there, Yale fraternities had less in common with the residential fraternities of state universities than they did with New York businessmen's clubs: at a certain hour on a weekday afternoon, a member could stroll in, order a gin-and-tonic from a black bartender who was wearing a white jacket, sign a chit for the drink, and repair for a game of pool or a snooze in a leather chair. (I believe that many undergraduates went through Yale under the vague impression that the liquor laws of Connecticut, which made it illegal to serve liquor to anyone under twenty-one, somehow didn't apply to, say, the bar at Zeta Psi.) When Farr arrived at Yale as a freshman, in 1892, the organizations that evolved into fraternities were junior societies—part of what I gathered had been a system of constant winnowing of the class that began with sophomore societies and ended on Tap Day with seventy-five members of the class being taken into senior societies. I have always remembered one anecdote he told me: Someone in his class who had been a member of a sophomore and junior society, and therefore would have been a good bet for a senior society, had not been tapped, Farr said, and had lived for the rest of his life in France because of the shame of it all.

The anecdote stuck with me partly, of course, because it was such an astounding example of the insane importance grown men could place on undergraduate goings-on. It conjured up images of a once patrician but now dissolute-looking expatriate in his sixties, drinking Pernod in a waterfront bar in Marseilles. "Don't you ever feel like going home?" an American traveler who happened to wander into the bar is saying to him. "Can't," the expatriate says, downing his Pernod. "Wasn't tapped." Partly, too, it made me realize that in the mind of someone from the Class of 1896 fraternities and senior societies and any other undergraduate institution must remain, to a large extent, what they were in 1896. Undergraduate views about what's important and what's not important in undergraduate life are hard to shake: to some extent, they remain the norm and everything else is a deviation. There was someone in my own class whose father, a graduate of Yale in the twenties, was reputed to have said to him as he left for New Haven, in the fall of 1953, not "Study hard" or "Make us proud" or "Be a gentleman" or "Write your mother" or (in the case of my own father) "You might as well be a mensch" but "My big mistake was turning down Wolf's Head and waiting for Bones." After I visited Yale in 1970, I was trying to explain to a classmate how the place had changed, and he said, "What's their word for weenie?" That was the point, I told him: they were so tolerant that they didn't have a word for weenie. He mulled that over for a few moments. "In that case," he finally said, "they're *all* weenies."

Also, I had to wonder whether the man who had lived in France for the rest of his life might have reasons other than Tap Day shame for being there. Of course, that might have been the genuine and only reason. Maybe an assiduous researcher could turn up letters from the expatriate that contained phrases like "Yes, I was saddened not to be able to return for my father's funeral, but I had to assume that Mutt Barnswell would be present, and I simply could not look him in the eye knowing that he knew how much I was counting on Book and Snake." But there are, after all, other reasons for living in France. Maybe, during a graduation tour of the Continent, he met a young woman from Dijon and found happiness running her family's mustard factory. Maybe he yearned for a life as a bohemian in Paris or as a student of French verb forms in Tours. It was certainly possible that what Tute Farr told me was simply the widespread interpretation in the Class of 1896 why this man would live abroad—the interpretation based on undergraduate views that were hard to shake even sixty years later. What occurred to me, as I made a pile of documents and family photographs and newspaper clippings to take to Denny's Aunt Norma, was that some of the people who had spoken at Tersh's may have been doing the equivalent when they analyzed Denny's life within the context of the promise and expectations connected with the college golden boy of the fifties. Many of the people in that room, after all, had been college golden boys in the fifties themselves; none of them had yet been elected President. It was natural for them to interpret Denny's life according to how closely it followed the trajectory that had been anticipated in college, just as it was natural for people in the Class of 1896 to assume that someone's entire life could be decided on Tap Day.

I had actually been surprised that the discussion at Tersh's turned out to be so analytical—what I had come to think of as the "Big Chill" session. I suppose it was natural for the conversation to have taken that turn, given the way Denny died and given the fact that many of the people in the room were analytical by nature and training and profession. But when Tersh said he was considering giving people an opportunity to say whatever they wanted to say about Denny, I had assumed, without giving it much thought, that what they would want to say would be mostly anecdotal. That's what it had been when my turn came. I told a couple of stories about Denny as a rube in Paris. I told a couple of stories about the time, just after graduation, when one of our friends from a shoe background got married and Denny and I took in the entire weekend's festivities. Among the gatherings was a wedding luncheon on the North Shore of Long Island given by, I think, the groom's grandmother, who lived in one of those grand houses with a vast lawn going down to the Sound. Denny and I were seated at different tables, but halfway through lunch he stopped behind me and whispered in my ear, "This is a house."

I was puzzled. "What are you talking about?" I whispered back.

"It's a house," he said. "I've just come from the john. There are personal pictures. It's a house."

"What'd you think it was?"

"I thought it was some kind of club," he said. I realized then that he was looking out for me: he wanted to save me the embarrassment of turning to the hostess and saying something like "Have you belonged here long?"

During the same weekend, we were all carted off to a debutante party, although I had no idea who the debutante was. The reception line had a sort of crier, who would take your name and then call it out to the debutante and her parents. Denny was in front of me. "Roger D. Hansen," he said. The crier said in orotund tones, "Roger D. Hansen." It was my turn. "Bud Trillin," I said, using the name just about everyone had called me since childhood. "Bud Trillin," the crier repeated. As we walked away, Denny turned to me and said, "Well! If there was one time to use Calvin, that was it."

I told some other stories about Denny, but they weren't illustrative of any theory about what might have happened in his life. They were just anecdotes. So what was I doing there, the day after his memorial service, in his house in Georgetown? Looking for more material for anecdotes? Just picking up some pictures and personal effects to take to Aunt Norma? I guess not. I wanted to know more about Denny. Poking around in other people's lives is nothing new for me, of course—I've done that for a living for a number of years—but ordinarily the people in question are strangers. This was something different, something quite a bit closer to those heart-to-hearts that my father—and I after him—had always tried to avoid. I hadn't been absolutely certain I was going to do it until after the gathering at Tersh's the night before—a gathering that had revealed a lot of things I hadn't known about Denny. Partly, I suppose, I had begun to wonder whether back in the fifties, when we had been under the impression that we were more or less in control of our futures, we might have made up a life for Denny to live.

Among the things I gathered up to take to California were some newspaper clippings reporting high-school swimming triumphs. Denny's swimming team was identified as the Sequoia Cherokees. It was a name, I thought, that would probably draw a murmured "Classic" from a student of fifties middle-class culture in America, although I would hardly qualify as an objective observer on that subject, since I myself had recorded the triumphs of the Southwest Indians in a yearbook called *The Sachem* and, at a Boy Scout camp called Camp Osceola, had become a brave in the Great Tribe of Mic-o-say.

There was an account of the meet at which the Sequoia Cherokees, led by the record-breaking relay team that Denny Hansen anchored, won the first North Coast Section championship that Sequoia High School had ever won. There was an account of the meet at which Sequoia, led by Art Lambert and Denny Hansen, beat Palo Alto High

School for the first time in nineteen years. Denny and his teammates were spectacular swimmers. As a senior, he was listed as a U.S. Junior Olympics Swimming Champion, with the country's best times in both the fifty-yard and fifty-meter freestyle. But what my attention fastened on, as I stood there in Denny's living room reading the clippings, was not a statistic but a passage from the Palo Alto account. Just after it reported that Denny had pulled the crowd to its feet in winning the fifty-yard freestyle in a brilliant 24.6, it said, "The chunky Cherokee a half-hour later unofficially broke the loops record for the 100 free." Chunky Cherokee! "Chunky Cherokee! Chunky Cherokee!" I called out to Tersh. "Why am I only learning this now, when it's too late?" We would have never let him forget Chunky Cherokee. It would have become an alternate name, used the way Eddie Williams used Eberhard Faber the Pencil King: "Could you please pass the salt to the Chunky Cherokee," or, years later, "I didn't know if you were already here so I asked the hostess if she had seated any Chunky Cherokees at a table for two." I thought, What a waste!—and then, my feelings triggered somehow by memories of silly undergraduate teasing, I realized how truly sad I was that my friend Denny had died, unhappy and alone, and how awful I felt that people who cared for him had not even known what was happening.

9

THERE were some items Tersh didn't know what to do with. He turned over to me a history of Scroll and Key and a register of Keys graduates that had been published in 1989. The fact that the register was still in its shrink wrap surprised me. I can't resist such books myself. Occasionally, as a weekend guest or a renter of a vacation cottage, I have found myself poring over volumes like *Princeton '52—Ten Years Out*, even though I don't know a soul involved. I actually own the Quindecennial Report of the Harvard Class of 1916. I was quite aware that Denny was not eager to drop in on anybody listed in the register, but I would have thought that, just as a matter of gossip fodder, he might have been curious. One member of our group, Bill Hall, had managed to get through to Denny not many months before, and they had talked amiably for a couple of hours. Bill was struck by two things: how intent Denny was about keeping his distance from us—Bill was conscious of being spoken to as someone who was calling long-distance rather than from a phone booth around the corner—and how genuinely pleased Denny had seemed to be by the opportunity to have a chat.

There was also a book called *A Register of Rhodes Scholars, 1903–1981*. It listed Rhodes Scholars by the year they were selected, in the style of *Who's Who*. Each person's listing included his father's name and occupation but no word at all of a mother, as if playing out some Shakespearean riddle about no man born of woman; the custom continued even after 1977, when some of the Rhodes Scholars listed were themselves women. The entry also listed what sort of degree each person got, and I saw that Denny's had been inflated a bit in the "Big Chill" session: he got a Second, which is what the bulk of American Rhodes Scholars seem to get. Some of the information about him was incorrect. It said that he was with the Potomac Associates—a place he had worked at briefly eight or nine years before the book was published. It also said that Denny was the son of "C. E. Hansen, attorney," and the *Life* piece had confirmed my memory that Denny's father, Clarence Hansen, was a former ship's officer who, by the time Denny was in high school, was working as an inspector for marine insurance companies. I took the errors to mean that Denny had treated requests for information from Oxford pretty much the way he treated requests for information from Yale.

Tersh and I decided that I could hold on to the Rhodes Scholar register for a while, and we packed up a lot of the other things to take to Aunt Norma. When it came to family for Denny in the last years of his life, I gathered, Aunt Norma had been about it. Denny's brother, Jerry, was only fourteen months older, but they had never been close—not childhood enemies but simply two boys with completely different interests. In the seventies, Denny had apparently had an angry falling out with his brother and his then sister-in-law over the subject that usually brings an angry falling out if there is one sibling who leaves and one who sticks close to home—responsibility for the care of aging parents and the control of their resources—and whatever tenuous contact had existed was broken. Denny had also lost touch with his mother, who was in a California nursing home but not considered lucid enough to be told of her son's death. One of the chilling facts about Denny's solitude that Tersh had mentioned during the gathering at his house was that the instructions left by Denny had mentioned that he was not certain whether his mother was dead or alive.

Aunt Norma was the last of her generation of Hansens, and as Tersh and I gathered up things at Denny's house, it occurred to me that some of the personal items I was taking to her—some early family pictures, for instance— might well have been sent by her to Denny in the first place after his father's death. I suspected that had been true of a picture book called *Windjammer* by the British writer Eric Newby. As a young man, Newby had shipped out on a huge, Finnish-built, four-masted barque called the *Moshulu* that—I was astonished to learn—was still hauling grain under sail from Australia to Great Britain as the Second World War approached. Apparently, the invention of machines to raise and lower sails meant that vast sailing ships could be operated by a tiny crew, and that a proprietor who had what Newby called an "obsessional interest in reducing running costs" could operate commercial transport vessels under sail long after the sort of activities popularly associated with sailing were afternoon outings in the harbor or charters in the Caribbean. An inscription on the inside page of the book said, " 'Moshulu'—last of the great barques. Under the command of Captain Lauritz C. Hansen when she was under West Coast ownership."

There were two or three oil paintings of large sailing ships in the living room—a rather formal room that didn't look particularly lived in. Except for a couple of huge, ornate mirrors, it had the sort of nondescript furniture that a competent decorator might have chosen for the rooms in a first-class hotel. Denny had presumably spent most of his time upstairs, in a bedroom and a large alcove that he had obviously used as an office. It was in the living room that he had left what passed for his suicide note—neatly stacked on top of some financial records on a table that held nothing else—before going off to Rehoboth Beach to die. The note —which, according to its date, had been begun a few months before—did mention his back pain. "I'm in a lot of pain, and will not consider further back surgery," he wrote. "The probabilities of any surgical relief are too marginal for me to hang on and suffer any more. When the pain becomes unbearable, I will take my own life. I will do so with regret, and with the feeling that there are no other viable options." On the whole, though, Denny left instructions rather than explanations. A sort of addendum that he headed "Some final ramblings" did not seem rambling at all. It provided, in a matter-of-fact tone, the name and address of the accountant who would have relevant financial documents and it reminded Tersh of a painting that was being held on consignment by a gallery in town.

10

THE pictures I packed up at Denny's house in George-town showed what seemed to be a family of fifties sit-com perfection—nice-looking parents, two clean-cut boys, neat California bungalow. But when I mentioned that to someone who had been one of Denny's closest friends at Yale, he said simply, "His family was not part of the whole thing." Denny's friends from various periods of his life all got the impression that he had not been raised in a home full of great nurturing and love. Clarence Hansen—one of five children of Lauritz Hansen, a Dane who ran off to sea as a boy and raised a family in Alameda, California, and became the last skipper of the *Moshulu*—was, according to what everyone who knew him says, a sweet, rather passive man who didn't have much to say. Denny's mother was what was then called nervous or high-strung and what might now be called manic-depressive, and she apparently had trouble getting along with all the Hansens clustered in the Bay Area. Denny's brother, Jerry, also swam for the Sequoia Cherokees, but he didn't produce the record-breaking performances that Denny managed—

not because he lacked natural talent, a couple of people told me, but because he didn't have the streak of perfectionism that kept Denny in the pool after everyone else had gone home. Jerry went to Cal Poly rather than Yale. His ex-wife, who still speaks of him as the "salt of the earth," says he was always more interested in his boat than his career, and he cheerfully agrees. For six or eight years he drove across the mountains every morning from Santa Cruz to Los Gatos, so he could continue to live close to the ocean while working in an aunt and uncle's auto supply shop; when they said that he should move into the community if he was going to take over the business someday, he quit. He worked as a mechanic in the Lipton tea factory near Santa Cruz for fifteen years, but always resented the six- and sometimes seven-day weeks that kept him off his boat, which he had begun sailing in trans-Pacific competitions. "Finally," he recalls, "I said, 'Wait a minute. Life's too short.' So I took early retirement, paid my boat off, and now I'm cruisin'." He's based in Hawaii. He has a 100-ton skipper's license with a sail endorsement—a third-generation Hansen mariner—and he sometimes finds work with parasail companies or booze cruises or harbor cruises or dive boats. When I spoke to him, he was thinking about going to Tahiti for a while. There's no telephone on his boat, and it had taken Tersh some time to satisfy himself that Jerry knew of his brother's death. Jerry and Denny hadn't spoken in perhaps a decade.

The book on the *Moshulu* had indeed been sent to Denny by his Aunt Norma. When I visited Norma Hansen in Los Gatos, I realized that even before she found herself the single survivor of Lauritz Hansen's children she had been more or less the keeper of the family history. Although the two principal documents of that history—the book on the *Moshulu* and the *Life* magazine issue that covered the graduation of Roger Dennis Hansen from Yale—are pretty impressive, the history itself is rather sparse. The Hansens did not proliferate in America. Aunt Norma's older brother—Denny's uncle, who worked as a San Francisco representative for a marine insurance company—died as a young man. Aunt Norma's two sisters were childless, and she never married. So the family contracted: Aunt Norma's generation began with five Hansens, but the third generation of the family in America consisted only of Clarence Hansen's two sons, Denny and Jerry. To some extent, that meant that the boys were the children of all the Hansens —after the bombing of Pearl Harbor, when there was a question of how safe Hawaii would be, they were sent to live for a few years with another aunt and her husband, who had a prune and apricot ranch in what is now Silicon Valley—but from what I had gathered, Aunt Norma was the only relative Denny had much contact with after he grew up. Denny's mother came from Southern California, from a family that was sparse and dispersed; her relatives didn't seem to figure at all in the lives of her sons. Aunt Norma may have been the relative Denny was closest to from childhood. She had, in fact, accompanied his parents to his graduation in 1957. We realized that we remembered each other from that weekend. At the time, she was working for the California Manufacturers Association in San Francisco, and was accustomed to traveling to Sacramento every year when the lobbyists visited legislators. She is retired now, but she remains vigorous—a direct, alert woman who still drives the spotless bronze-and-black Mercury Cougar she bought new in 1968. When I saw her in California, she told me that she and Denny used to joke a lot, and that she was shocked when he wrote her a few years ago, during a blue period, and said that he had experienced periods of depression even as early as his years at Yale.

In the fifties, I think, it was common for a young man like Denny or like me—someone whose grandparents had been immigrants and whose family hadn't been to college—to be sent away to places like Yale by parents who realized that they were putting a distance between themselves and their son forever, whether he eventually returned to live in his hometown or not. I know that my father was aware of that from the start, because after he died, my mother told me so, not without a touch of resentment. Still, it's hard for me to think of anyone I've known who became completely cut off from the people who raised him—what the social scientists would call his family of origin. I can think of some people whose contact was almost entirely irritating or even painful, but there was contact. In fact, when I reached a certain age, around my late thirties or early forties, it even occurred to me that one elemental fact of life separating the people I knew into groups had to do with their relationship with their family of origin: those who, in one way or another, took care of their parents and those whose parents still more or less took care of them. I don't think it occurred to me at the time that I knew anyone whose contact with the people who had raised him was so slight that he would belong in neither category. Some of the pictures at Denny's house showed him back home on family visits in the years after he moved to Washington, but his brother, Jerry, summed up what must have been the view from California in one sentence, without sounding at all put out: "He went off to college by himself and no one ever saw him again."

I find it even more difficult to conceive of someone in college having such a slight connection with his family that it could be said, "His family was not part of the whole thing." That may be because it isn't easy for me to imagine my life without my family—particularly without my father's aspirations. It always seemed to me that people who come from immigrant families in America—people who Tom Regan in *Stover at Yale* might have described, as he described himself, as having "come from nothing"—are as much captives of their families as people who are always talking about family traditions that date back to colonial days. There's no question of the sacrifices made for you having faded from memory. On that graduation weekend when I met Aunt Norma and Denny's parents, I may have simply assumed that all of us whose families did not take something like graduation from college for granted were at Yale partly because they had fathers something like my father.

Since 1988, I have gone to graduation every May. I march in the procession as a member of the board of trustees—what's called at Yale the Corporation. I was elected to the Corporation by the alumni in a process that did not overtly forbid campaigning but ruled it out with a phrase that snapped me back to the fifties: "It's been traditional not to." My presence on the Yale Corporation sometimes strikes me as odd—unlike my fellow trustees,

most of whom are laden with directorships and trustee-
ships, my previous experience in such matters was the parents' committee of P.S. 3—but for all I know, it was part
of my father's plan from the start. I assume that he would
take my own children's attendance at Yale for granted as
part of the plan, and he was, of course, in my mind the
weekend my older daughter graduated. But I find that I
always think of him during commencement weekend, particularly when I see a black family there to celebrate the
graduation of a son or daughter. It seems to me that black
families tend to arrive in great profusion—not just parents
but aunts and uncles and grandparents and great-aunts. I
figure that the person graduating, having drawn a crowd
like that, can have no doubts at all that he or she comes
from something, just as I did when my parents came that
weekend in 1957 and my dad commented wryly to Denny
on my lack of reverence in the Class History.

I don't mean that Denny's parents weren't proud of him
or that he had no affection for them. But from what people
who knew him and his family say, I'm not sure that he felt
that his presence there—on the Old Campus, holding the
class banner—flowed from them. Of course they were
proud of him. They must have been terribly proud when
the piece in *Life* appeared. In fact, the whole South Bay
must have been terribly proud. Somebody I visited in California gave me a clipping from an issue of the Redwood
City *Tribune* dated a couple of weeks after the *Life* piece.
It was a letter to the editor in which a local woman said
that she had read with great dismay about a group of local
boys attacking some Stanford students and had then picked

up "this week's *Life* magazine and read of the doings of another local Peninsula boy, Roger Dennis Hansen, graduate with honors from Yale." Reflecting a line from the letter, the headline read, SHE THANKS GOD FOR ROGER HANSEN.

11

EISENSTAEDT had been hoping for a cover, Steve Kezerian told me. Kezerian, who is retired now, was the
director of the Yale University News Bureau at the time.
To the people at *Life*, the piece on Denny Hansen's graduation was pretty routine—what Michael Arlen, when I
asked him about it, called "expanded rotogravure stuff."
But for somebody whose job it was to disseminate news
of Yale to the outside world it had to be one of the high
points—a jackpot of glowing publicity in the single best
outlet then available in America. By 1957, Kezerian told
me, he had got into the habit of sending memos to education editors in New York—*The New York Times* and
the newsmagazines and especially *Life* were the most important targets—and then taking the train down to Man-
hattan to see if anybody had bitten. Often, nobody had.
The president of Yale, A. Whitney Griswold, was talking
a lot about liberal arts, and, Kezerian reminded me,
"there's nothing sexy about liberal arts." In the early spring
of 1957, Kezerian walked in to see Edward Kern, the education editor of *Life*, about the suggestions he had sent

a week or two before. "He said they really liked my suggestion of covering graduation by following around one student," Kezerian told me. "Give me this much credit, Bud: my jaw didn't drop. Because I hadn't sent in anything like that. I didn't say that, of course. What I said was 'I'm glad you like it, Ed.' " Kezerian later asked around among his counterparts at other schools, and decided that the commencement-story idea might have come from Amherst and somehow lost its source.

In those years Yale had on hand not only some gentlemen professors but what amounted to some gentlemen administrators—people with deep Yale credentials who had returned after some years in private business to work at the university, often in the development office. The man in Griswold's administration whose responsibilities included oversight of the News Bureau was one of those—Carlos P. Stoddard, known as Totty, whose experience in journalism was as the chairman of the *Yale Daily News*, Class of 1926. In the Yale of the twenties, that position would have been thought of as presaging not a career in the press, an enterprise that remained déclassé at least through the fifties, but a tap by both Bones and Keys. Stoddard, as it happened, had gone Keys, and he was among the people in the faculty and administration who kept an eye on the place—in his case, literally as well as figuratively, since his office in Woodbridge Hall overlooked the flower garden in the back of the Keys tomb. When I went back to Yale in the hectic days of 1970, I happened to run into him on the street, and he told me, shaking his head in sadness and puzzlement, that the seniors in Keys then were quite a different sort of crowd than we had been.

"You know what they told me?" he said. "They told me the Keys garden is elitist."

It seemed a bit late for Totty Stoddard and me to go into the matter of elitism, a word that was unknown in 1957, let alone 1926. (Even in 1957, if somebody had defined "elitism" for us, he would have had to spend some more time explaining why it was meant pejoratively.) "The Keys garden is supposed to be elitist, Mr. Stoddard," I said, trying to cheer him up. "I don't think you should worry about that."

It was up to the university to provide a graduating senior to build the *Life* commencement story around, and Kezerian met with Stoddard and Stoddard's deputy to talk about which undergraduate would be served up. What they had in mind was someone who personified the broadening access to Yale—a "real American," and preferably one who was what would these days be called a scholar-athlete. They wanted a public-school boy from the West—although I realized that their idea of the West and mine might be somewhat different when Kezerian said that one place the Western requirement brought to mind was Cincinnati. "Tot said, 'Let me see here,' " Kezerian told me. "He was looking down at his desk. And I became very much aware that he was going down the Keys list." Almost immediately, Stoddard came across a perfect example of a Western, real-American scholar-athlete—Denny Hansen. As a matter of fairness and diplomacy, Kezerian said, Stoddard decided to send *Life* the name of somebody from Bones as well. I can't imagine that there had been any undergraduates in years who viewed the world as divided essentially between Bones and Keys. But Totty Stoddard's definitions of what constituted fairness in such matters had been formed in the Class of 1926, and I'm confident that he was always true to them.

The Bones man was a fullback named Steve Ackerman, who didn't actually seem to fit the profile Stoddard was looking for. He had gone to Lawrenceville, although he wasn't from a shoe family. Also, he was from the East. Also—Kezerian remembers this being in the air—the name Ackerman could be Jewish, although in Steve's case it's Dutch. Everybody who was involved in press relations in colleges like Yale, Kezerian told me, was aware of what had happened to Wellesley a couple of years before this. *Life* had decided to visit the annual event at which fathers come to Wellesley for a weekend of activities with their sophomore daughters. The press people at Wellesley had thought that they had hit the jackpot. But when the story came out, Kezerian said, word went around the loose fraternity of Eastern college press relations people that Wellesley considered it a disastrous backfire: it happened to feature some fathers with Jewish names, and Wellesley felt in danger of being typed as a "Jewish school."

There wasn't much chance that Steve Ackerman would be in *Life* anyway. Apparently, he was held in reserve as a sort of alternate, in case Denny didn't work out. I suppose a cynic could say that Totty Stoddard's notion of being fair by 1926 standards did not extend to including the name of a Bones man who was actually likely to be chosen. Although the method of choosing our class's most compelling hero may have come out of another era—the scene in Stoddard's office could almost have been written by Owen Johnson, except that his rendition would have had

Stoddard murmuring, as he came across Denny's name, "Solid chap, Hansen"—I have to say that an objective committee might well have come to the same conclusion. It wouldn't have been the obvious call that it might have been at Sequoia High School: undergraduate life at Yale was not organized in a way that was likely to produce one student who was known by face and name to all others. I don't doubt that any number of people in our class would have had trouble placing the person carrying the 1957 banner into the Old Campus at commencement. But Denny did have that stunning completeness. He was a varsity athlete, although, competing on the only team at Yale that was nationally ranked, not really a star athlete. He was from a public high school in the West. He had the dazzling smile. He looked like a modern Frank Merriwell, the Yale hero who always managed to save the game, although Kezerian remembers suggesting to him that he drop a few pounds before Eisenstaedt showed up. Also, Denny came equipped with the one unmatchable shorthand label of college success: he was a Rhodes Scholar. The other Rhodes Scholar in our class (aside from someone who had joined us only senior year) was Erwin Fleissner, whose undergraduate career had a certain completeness of its own: he was a physics and philosophy major who had won English prizes and played intermural squash and soccer. But Erwin was a quiet fellow from New York State, and had been to boarding school, and had a name that, I suppose, could have reminded everyone how the Wellesley jackpot had turned out to be of valueless coin.

So *Life* did Denny, maybe by accident. Kezerian got a raise. He told me that Whitney Griswold seemed to like the piece until his summer neighbor on Martha's Vineyard, Kingman Brewster, who was then the dean of Harvard Law School, started kidding him about the final picture, which shows Denny with Robert Kiphuth, the swimming coach who was responsible for Yale's unlikely prominence in the sport. ("This is a very satisfying sport as Yale never loses," the authors of "Inside Eli" wrote. "Only swimmers speak to Kiphuth and Kiphuth speaks only to God.") The picture carries a caption that says, "Hansen said goodbye to the man who, he says, had done more for him at Yale than anyone else." As Kezerian heard the story, Brewster's banter went something like this: "The guy who did the most for him was a swimming coach! Don't you have any professors in that place anymore?" After that, according to Kezerian, Griswold seemed to include the *Life* piece in the sort of coverage of Yale he sometimes referred to as "all that Frank Merriwell crap."

Of course, a lot of Denny's friends came to believe that he would have been a lot better off in the long run if Totty Stoddard hadn't picked his name off the Keys list, or if the *Life* team had gone to Amherst, where it might have been meant to go—leaving Denny without the sort of attention that produces headlines like SHE THANKS GOD FOR ROGER HANSEN. The *Life* piece, some people think, put Denny's youthful promise in indelible ink, for all the world to see, and after that there was no escaping it. "*Life* was probably right: he was a symbol of what we were," Tersh Boasberg said to me on the telephone a few days after Denny died. "And in a way that was the worst thing that could have happened to him." Joe Clayton, writing a month or so after the memorial service to the secretary of Denny's Rhodes class—Don Smith, an historian who teaches at Grinnell College—said that he didn't think Denny's separation from his old friends in the eighties was the result of a "change of lifestyle" but of "his inability to cope with a career which, slipping, did not match the heroic, larger-than-life image which was created in California and nurtured in New Haven." In that letter, Joe said that Yale might have been unfair to Denny. Needing "a high school hero to change and nationalize the old boy image of the past," he wrote, Yale "thrust him into a position which he could not sustain. He had no underpinnings: no family stability, no cultural perspective, and, essentially, no roots."

I looked up the *Life* piece on Wellesley. It was headlined BIG DATE WITH DADDY. The lead picture—almost a full page—was of two fathers wearing Wellesley beanies. One of them had a name that might have been Jewish or might not have been. The other one was named Irving Goldstein. Most of the people in the story—like most of the people at Wellesley, I presume—had names like Burke and Browning. There must have been a feeling in the fifties that you couldn't be too careful: one Irving Goldstein might do it. At *Life*, I also looked up the contact sheets of the many rolls of film Alfred Eisenstaedt had taken that weekend. There were shots of Denny draping the class flag over the stage at commencement, and of Denny getting his diploma at the smaller ceremony in the courtyard of our residential college, and of Dean Acheson, then the senior fellow of the Yale Corporation, wearing a magnificent floppy hat that he must have picked up with an honorary degree from Oxford or Cambridge, and of the procession into the Old Campus, with Corporation members and honorary degree recipients following Whitney Griswold. Dag Hammarskjöld, the Secretary-General of the United Nations, and Robert Goheen, then the new president of Princeton, were the only honorary degree recipients I recognized. When I looked up the full list, my instant impression, from the vantage point of someone who has to be concerned with honorary degrees in the early nineties, was "My God! Thirteen males!"

There were also a lot of shots of Denny with his date for the weekend, identified as "Smith sophomore Sue Kirk." It had been mentioned at Tersh's that at the time Sue was actually going out with Pudge Henkel; the commencement weekend was in the nature of temporary duty because of the *Life* piece. Still, Sue and Denny made a handsome couple—the Denny smile seemed particularly glowing when they were seen together—and a few of the shots struck me as having the same youthful exuberance as the shot of Denny and the to-die-for Marilyn Montgomery. "Denny was totally comfortable with it," Sue said, when I asked her many years later about being followed around by the *Life* crew that weekend. "When I got off the train, this little minnow of a man popped up and started taking pictures, and he kept it up the whole weekend. Denny said, 'Just don't pay any attention to it,' and *he* didn't. He was completely natural. I was conscious of it the whole time." Near the end of the contact sheets, I came across the shot I realized I had been hoping to find—the one of Denny at the Class Day ceremony. It had been taken well before the ceremony started. There were only half a dozen people in the vast sea of folding chairs that had been set up on the Old Campus. Seated together in the front row were Mike Dodge, Denny, and my father.

12

HOWARD Lamar, a soft-spoken historian of the American West, spent more than forty years on the Yale faculty, including several years as dean of Yale College, and, at the close of his career, he agreed to serve a year as acting president of the university. He was Denny's mentor at Yale, and according to friends of Denny's in Washington, he had remained among the people Denny continued to respect without qualification—a list that got increasingly difficult to stay on over the years. When I visited Lamar to talk about Denny, he remarked that Yale in our day, aside from the skewed admissions system, had a sort of "youthful meritocracy" once you got in—a willingness to grant "acceptance regardless of who you were." In our era, a lot of the undergraduate energy—academic and athletic and extracurricular—was provided by the new people, and it's true that the captain of the football team was assumed to be an automatic tap for Bones whether he had an Eastern European name or not.

Of course, the captain of Dink Stover's team, Tom Regan, who "came from nothing," had also been tapped for

Bones. When Dink and his friend Tough McCarthy pass an ominous-looking society tomb early in their freshman year and McCarthy comments on how scary it looks, Stover says, "It stands for democracy, Tough." In Stover's view, it stood for democracy because it was a badge of success open to anyone who proved himself—anyone who rose in the youthful meritocracy. (Dink's quarrel was with the sophomore societies, partly because their selection had to be based largely on background and connections.) By the time Denny and I arrived, Yale didn't have much resemblance on the surface to the place my father had read about in *Stover at Yale*, but the more I think about it, the more I think that we were closer to the world inhabited by Dink and Tough than we were to the world of today's Yale undergraduates. Shortly after Denny and I arrived in New Haven, a committee on general education, chaired by A. Whitney Griswold himself, maintained that Yale education remained hampered by "a false myth of Yale—the Yale of casual but big-time activity, the Yale glorified and made famous by Owen Johnson and the rest." I think the report was correct in its assumption that—despite the upheavals of the Second World War and the influx of people like Denny and me, despite the fact that Tute Farr's story about an untapped senior's lifetime exile to the Continent sounded as bizarre then as it does today—a diluted form of the system Stover found in New Haven still existed. Contrary to what the Freshman Office was saying about the importance of intellectual opportunities, "Inside Eli" said it was offering freshmen a tout sheet on extracurricular activities because "what you really want to know is how to get on in the great Yale Game." I remember writing an editorial not long before that informing incoming freshmen that "Yale is not a game to beat, a system to figure out, a world to conquer," but I also remember that I didn't truly believe it when I wrote it.

By the time we were at Yale, Tap Day—the central metaphor for what Bob Mason had described that night at Tersh's as our tendency to make people into winners or losers—had been criticized for years. But a tap from a senior society remained a basic form of recognition in our lives, as it had been in Stover's, whether the person tapped wanted to join a society or not. ("People in houses without any windows," I wrote in the Class History, "don't give a damn about stones.") The fact that the most coveted societies seemed organized around the premise that there was some purpose served in arranging for, say, a star lacrosse player and a classics scholar and the alto from a singing group and the editor of the humor magazine to spend several hours together every week, without much regard for whether any of them got to Yale by family tradition or bread-company rebate, meant that you could see the system as democratic. It also meant that absolutely everybody was being judged. The elements that finally removed the spring from the tightly wound little world of undergraduate Yale didn't come together until a dozen years after Denny and I left: the radically changed outlook of students in the late sixties and the advent of co-education. "With girls around," one of my classmates observed, "you couldn't do any of that stuff with a straight face."

"Yale was seen as more elite and different then," Lamar told me. "So when Yale accepted you it made you even more nervous. I always thought the loyalty of alumni to

Yale was all the fiercer because it is tinged with doubt." It's true that what overtly non-shoe freshmen found intimidating was mainly just a matter of style, and for most people, I think, the feeling of being in a foreign place had evaporated within the first year. From what I gathered from Lamar and some of the people in our class who had known Denny as a freshman, though, that first year must have seemed to him to last forever. For much of it, apparently, Denny had been miserable and homesick, although not literally longing for his own home, since, in Lamar's view, "it was almost as if his high-school experience was more real than his family—he was bound in his generation." When Denny wasn't circulating on the Old Campus, flashing his astonishing smile, he might have been in his room, lonely and sad and sometimes seriously depressed. He found a lot to complain about. He thought that a number of people in the class—maybe the last ten or fifteen of those sixty-two people from Andover, as an example— really didn't belong at Yale. He had some aches and pains. Sometimes, though, he must have had low periods that weren't specifically connected to being away from home or being concerned about how he was faring on the swimming team or being irritated by the admissions system. From talking to people who knew him then and later, I'm convinced that even at that age Denny had black moods that were unexplained and maybe inexplicable.

But all of that would have seemed unlikely for anybody who ran across Denny in a crowd. "The atmosphere was so reassuring," I was told by Lamar, who met Denny in the fall of 1954, in a history seminar Lamar offered for sophomores in our residential college. "His native abilities.

His California presence. He reassured us and we reassured him." Jay Inglis, who was one of Denny's closest friends at Yale, thinks that Denny came to look on his success in a crowd as suspect. "I think he had expectations that he would succeed as a swimmer at Yale, and when he found he couldn't hold his own, that had a negative impact," Jay told me one day when we had lunch to talk about Denny. "He knew he was very bright, but it turned out that he was not just very bright but one of the top people in the class. He became more concerned with the intellectual side, more driven. He had an incredible ability to be charming when he was Denny, and I think he enjoyed it. He enjoyed people. But the fact that he could maneuver very well—that he had this charm and personality—was opposed to the intellectual side of his life, and he turned it into a negative. He became very critical of the kind of person he really was—a person with the ability to be charming, what he called fluff." If that theory is correct, the side of Denny that made him so memorable to our parents—the side of him, for that matter, that led to our discussing our roles in his Administration—was a side that he came to look down on. From the conversations I had after Denny's death, it's clear to me that any colleague of his who could be described as smooth or charming or well connected was certain to be a colleague he loathed.

People such as Howard Lamar understood that at Yale Denny was never truly reassured. Apparently, he felt unworthy—as if, after each challenge was met, he believed that he had somehow got away with it once again but that they were sure to catch up with him the next time. Psychiatrists sometimes call that pattern an impostor complex.

It's a condition that can strike a layman as not so far from the way a balanced and sensible and reasonably modest person would think. "Which successful person does not have that feeling at times?" I was asked by a distinguished academic when I mentioned the impostor complex. No doubts? No understanding that a lot of it was luck? What can seem like pathology in someone who has achieved success in one field or another is the opposite of an impostor complex—being so swollen with ego that you don't have any doubts at all.

I suppose you could argue that a tendency to doubt success might have been one reason that Denny was interested in succeeding in swimming. When you win a swimming event there is no way to question whether you're worthy of winning or whether you might be credited with more talent than you really have: if you get to the end of the pool first, you win. But Denny's teachers had no doubts about his academic abilities, either. Howard Lamar was immediately struck by Denny's performance in his sophomore history seminar. "In class, two qualities always astounded me," Lamar told me. "One was his sense of discovery. The other was that he would often question the logic of something. He would start questioning something, very gently, but with impeccable logic. You'd say that Buchanan was, all in all, a terrible President, and he'd say, 'But he had some impossible problems,' and sooner or later you'd find yourself feeling sorry for Buchanan. He always managed to see it in an objective way, and he analyzed himself that way."

Still, Howard Lamar never thought Denny would become an academic. He took it for granted that the charm would lead to a career in politics. And he was never certain that Denny was very comfortable in the role of an academic, even after *The Politics of Mexican Development* was published. "He sent me his first book," Lamar said. "I felt it wasn't the real Denny writing the book. It was a book a scholar of international relations would write. But it was written almost as if he was wearing a formal mask. The exuberance was not there." Lamar, like the rest of us, had seen Denny rarely in recent years. As far as I could tell, Denny had maintained virtually no connection with Yale except for one visit that Lamar recalled: "He came here to give some talks, maybe ten years ago. He was his old self for an evening. I drove him to where he was staying. The talk had gone well, and in the dark of the car, he just talked, talked, talked. After that, there was silence. That evening was like a reprise in a Broadway show—doing the nice parts again."

13

_____

ROBERT Rotberg, who was in the 1957 class of Rhodes
Scholars with Denny and is now the president of La-
fayette College, wrote (with the collaboration of Miles F.
Shore) a biography of Cecil Rhodes called *The Founder*.
In its closing chapters, it traces the steps in Rhodes's thinking that led to the Rhodes Scholarships. The second of
many versions of Cecil Rhodes's will, Rotberg wrote, left
his assets to a secret society: "That Masonic, Jesuit-like
entity would have had as its object the extension of British
rule and emigration throughout the globe, the reattachment
of the United States to the empire, and the 'foundation of
so great a power as to . . . render wars impossible and
promote the best interests of humanity.' " The sixth and
seventh versions would have left part of the Rhodes estate
to found a college in Cape Town modeled on Oxford and
Cambridge. Then Rhodes was apparently influenced by the
ideas of two men in England who proposed a scholarship
to Oxford that would strengthen "those invisible ties,
stronger than any which can be devised by the cunning of
lawmakers, which will keep together, for good or ill, the

Anglo-Saxon race." In his final will, Rhodes said, "My desire being that the students who shall be elected to the Scholarships shall not be merely bookworms, I direct that in the election of a student to a Scholarship regard shall be had to (i) his literary and scholastic attainments, (ii) his fondness of and success in manly outdoor sports such as cricket, football and the like, (iii) his qualities of manhood, truth, courage, devotion to duty, sympathy for and protection of the weak, kindliness, unselfishness, and fellowship, and (iv) his exhibition during school days of moral force, of character and of instincts to lead and to take an interest in his schoolmates, for those latter attributes will be likely in afterlife to guide him to esteem the performance of public duties as his highest aim." In Rotberg's view, the notion of a Masonic-like order remained part of Cecil Rhodes's views of the scholarship. Rhodes saw the men chosen as people who would forge a bond with one another and help one another personally and professionally—not merely to promote the empire and the Anglo-Saxon race but to get things done wherever they were. (The tendency of Bill Clinton, Rhodes Class of 1968, to draw on a network of fellow Rhodes Scholars is apparently just the sort of thing Cecil Rhodes had in mind.) In what became the best-known description of what Rhodes had in mind, he said in a letter that the sort of person he was looking for was "the best man for the world's fight."

In the United States, which has sent thirty-two Rhodes Scholars to Oxford every year since 1904, it is assumed by now that the people chosen will concentrate on their own battles, and that the scholarship has given them for that purpose either a leg up or a great burden. A Rhodes Scholarship is, in the words of Michael Kinsley, of *The New Republic*, who was awarded one in 1972, "the ultimate ticket punch"—the one college-age credential that someone carries with him all through life, long after the eighty-yard run and the valedictorian's speech are forgotten. I have heard it said that the only two things you can do at the age of twenty-one that will become part of your identification permanently are win a Rhodes Scholarship or join the Marines. For people fixated on their resumés, Kinsley told me, being awarded a Rhodes Scholarship means that you don't have to go to law school—although he estimated that about half his group went to law school anyway—or that if you do go to law school you don't have to make Law Review. In our era, it meant pretty much of an automatic job offer from a corporation like Time Inc. It can also mean that everything from then on is thought of as a bit of a letdown, by the Rhodes Scholar and by those who know him. Someone who was a Rhodes Scholar with Denny told me, "One of the things Rhodes Scholars are subject to is the inability to be the world's best person, the best man to do the world's work. When you're twenty-one, you think you are."

As far as I can discover, there has never been a serious study to find out how Rhodes Scholars fare in later life, as compared to, say, people who are awarded other scholarships for study abroad, such as the Marshall or the Henry or (in the case of Yale) the Clare. A study of Rhodes Scholars strikes me as a ready-made project for some social scientist: *The American Oxonian*, a quarterly published by the American Association of Rhodes Scholars, even furnishes a list of names and addresses annually. (For twenty-five dollars, Americans who went to Oxford but were not Rhodes Scholars can be included in a separate listing.) Of course, even if the social scientist knew what he was looking for—promise fulfilled? some sort of victory in the world's fight?—there would be variables to control. How much of what happens to Rhodes Scholars in later life has to do with the judgment of the selection committee and how much with the fact that Rhodes Scholar became part of their identification? And what is the criterion for, say, promise fulfilled? A listing in *Who's Who*? A listing in the issue *Forbes* devotes annually to the richest people in America? Election to the American Academy of Arts and Sciences? A seat in the Senate? A lifetime of service? A ticket that has been punched so many times that it's practically in tatters?

I did run across a *Rhodes Scholar Career Census* that was published in 1988 as a sort of sidebar to a piece that *Spy* ran about Rhodes Scholars and introduced with a sentence indicating that what followed might not be altogether friendly: "Rhodes Scholars are the apotheosis of the hustling apple-polisher, the triumph of the resumé-obsessed goody-goody, the epitome of the blue-chip nincompoop." The author, Andrew Sullivan, a British graduate of Oxford who later became the editor of *The New Republic*, presented some calculations arranged in rough categories like lawyer and journalist and "academic in non-top-ten school" and "academic in top-ten school" and United States senator. Among the Rhodes Scholars I spoke to in Washington after Denny's death, there seemed to be a concentration of interest in the last category. At the time, there were five Rhodes Scholars in the Senate, although more than one person expressed the total to me by saying, "Five if you count Larry Pressler." Sullivan dismissed Pressler, of South Dakota, as a lightweight who was known as Larry Press Release. Although the other four were described by Sullivan as "unctuous and overrated" senators with "safe establishment convictions," they are sometimes described by others as senators of particular substance: David Boren, Paul Sarbanes, Bill Bradley, and Richard Lugar. The unkindest cut Sullivan got in about Rhodes Scholars in politics was a theory that was soon destroyed by Bill Clinton: that there would never be a Rhodes Scholar in the White House because the presidency is not an appointive office.

One of the problems that a Rhodes Scholar carries with him, of course, is that a senator is what a lot of people expect him to be—even though until 1976 J. William Fulbright was the only Rhodes Scholar who had ever been one. I'm not sure that the Rhodes Scholars of our era necessarily had those sorts of expectations for themselves. In 1957, before transatlantic jet travel became routine, being sent to England for two years—and, it was assumed, to the Continent in those long Oxford breaks—represented for most people an extraordinary adventure as much as it did an extraordinary honor. Reading about the counsellors provided by some universities these days to work with prospective Rhodes Scholars on honing essays and preparing for interviews, I realize that we emerged from college in an era of almost Stoveresque amateurism—before absolutely anything a young American might compete for, from a beauty pageant to the 4-H steer competition at a livestock show, became surrounded with professional crammers and coaches and consultants. I suspect that any number of Rhodes Scholars of our era are leading productive and satisfying lives as, say, doctors or lawyers or academics in non-top-ten schools, and think of their selection thirty or forty years ago as simply a piece of good fortune that permitted them to have a useful academic experience at Oxford and some youthful flings in France and Italy that they would have otherwise missed. The other Rhodes Scholar from our class, Erwin Fleissner, who spent many years as a cancer researcher at Sloan-Kettering and then became dean of sciences at Hunter College, in New York, certainly seems to feel that way. There are obviously others, though, who have been conscious of the knapsack full of promise they have had to lug around. "It's hard to find the ability to let go," I was told by Frank Sieverts, a Rhodes Scholar I know who went to Oxford in 1955 and was in the State Department for a number of years and now works for the Senate Foreign Relations Committee. "A lot of people of our generation don't find a way to break the pattern. They carry a heavy burden, and the burden is reinforced by what people expect of them. You have to find a way to break the pattern."

I happen to know two or three people who were in the Rhodes Class of 1957 with Denny, but otherwise I wouldn't have recognized any of the names listed under 1957 in the register I found in his house. (On the other hand, among those appearing on one page in the listing for the Class of 1958 were the writer Jonathan Kozol, the singer and actor Kris Kristofferson, and Jason McManus, the editor in chief of Time Warner.) Going through the 1957 list, what I found surprising, considering the way Cecil Rhodes felt about bookworms, is how many academics there were—roughly two-thirds by my count. By 1960, a year after most of those in the group had left Oxford, Dick Pfaff, who served as Class Secretary for the first fifteen or so years out, began his class letter in *The American Oxonian* by saying, "The Class of 1957 seems distinguished chiefly by a disinclination to do anything besides pottering around various academic places," and the letter could have begun that way thirty years later.

I think that a lot of members of the Class of 1957, including Denny, had arrived at Oxford without an academic career in mind. At Oxford, though, as one of them told me, "one of the things that can happen is that you're exposed to a good faculty and you see scholarly life as comfortable. You start to think the disinterested search for truth is here embodied. Everything else is hustle and bustle. You may lose a kind of conventional professional ambition and take on a kind of dreaminess." André Schiffrin, who was at Cambridge on a Clare fellowship while Denny was at Oxford, wrote some years later that he and his fellow Americans had prepared for their second winter in England "as Admiral Perry must have," but he also wrote that "apart from the cold, life was extraordinarily graceful." A student at Oxford or Cambridge had his own suite of rooms. He had the services of someone who bore some resemblance to a manservant. He had a certain station. The life of the tutors could strike a Rhodes Scholar as even more graceful—unhurried, civilized, seemingly rarefied beyond concerns of career or advancement. It was an appealing model, even if it didn't have much to do with the life of an academic in the United States.

In Jason McManus's view, some Rhodes Scholars may

have become more involved in the academic than they had expected to partly because the alternative activities that had kept them busy enough at Yale or Ohio State or West Point to impress the Rhodes selection committee were not immediately available. Rhodes Scholars often found themselves outsiders when they got to Oxford. British students were a different age and came from a different background and often affected a certain disdain for colonials. "Denny is a bit cold—he didn't come off very well in the room assignments—and a bit lonely," I reported in a letter home to my parents, after I returned to London from a visit to Oxford. "I think it's a little hard to 'break in' with the British . . . but I think that's fairly natural at first for an American—especially someone who is so American and so outgoing." In the fifties, a lot of people in England were finally coming to grips with the fact that the empire was no more, and particularly after the United States failed to back the British and French adventure at Suez, there was a lot of resentment of American wealth and American power. I was on the Underground in London the day the first American attempt to send a rocket into space fizzled on the launch pad, and the atmosphere was similar to the atmosphere on the morning after England had won an important test match. Even in the days before the United States became so patently too big for its britches, I suspect, not a lot of those handwritten invitations for tea two weeks hence had gone to newly arrived Americans.

Whether they felt like outsiders or not, a lot of Americans apparently felt liberated from the pressure to demonstrate their stunning completeness. "I realized the degree to which Yale had resembled a job, how much it had fitted into the

American pattern of effort and reward," André Schiffrin wrote. "Here I did what I wanted because I wanted to . . . The books that I had always wanted to read and had always put off could now be read. The new books that tempted me succeeded in seducing me, and not only could I read them, I could persuade others to read them and could discuss them with my supervisor. I realized only later what this meant in terms of building an intellectual. We were all of us free—we could all have the time. Even the dons were not so tied to their research and publishing that they could not join us."

For one reason or the other, a lot of Rhodes Scholars of that era channeled their fearsome energy into scholarship, and went on to graduate school. Even if they didn't think scholarship would be their life's work, those who were beginning to have the normal concerns about what they might choose to do in the world of hustle and bustle knew that there was one thing they were definitely good at—going to school. Also, any male who had been to graduate school for a couple of years could put in a couple of more and be too old to worry about the draft. All in all, graduate school was a logical first step after Oxford for a lot of people in the Rhodes Class of 1957, and it appears that almost everyone who took it went on to lead the life of an academic. From the beginning, the Class of 1957 letter in *The American Oxonian* was dominated by the climb through academia—someone moving to Harvard to be associate professor of classics, someone writing the secretary from a conference on the historical relations between East Africa and the Orient before 1500, somebody going to the physics department of Pacific Lutheran University in Tacoma.

Denny was not a regular in the letters, but for some years he showed up now and then. "HANSEN finished the Woodrow Wilson School at Princeton with a Master's degree in Public and International Administration. Subsequent plans were not finally decided on when this was written," the letter reported in 1961. The following year, it said that he had left the staff of Senator Harrison Williams, of New Jersey, and joined NBC News. In 1970, there was an item that said, "HANSEN responded to the secretary's request in tabular form: 'An account of my life: uneventful. My opinions: perverse. My increasings: You ask this question with the Dow Jones passing 723 on the way down. My decrepitudes: they are my only increasings. Arthritis, receding hairline, yearly physicals, etc. But all is not lost. Washington visits from Smith, Rotberg, and Johnson cheered me. My own salient (and sole) accomplishment remains prospective: Johns Hopkins Press will publish my study of Mexico later this fall. Presumably it will be titled *The Politics of Mexican Development*. A shorter and incredibly sanitized version of it will also be published by the National Planning Association, with whom I still earn my livelihood."

The following year, the secretary was able to include a fairly full report of Denny's professional activities: "HANSEN is moving to a new job which sounds so much like a front for the C.I.A. that it cannot possibly be: 'Since last June, I have been working on the Staff of the President's Commission on International Trade and Investment Policy. The report of the Commission should be in final draft by June, and I'll be on my way to a new job on July 1. I have joined a new outfit in Washington called Potomac Associates, assuming the rather enigmatic title of Senior Associate. If I really knew what I would be doing there I'd tell you, but since the organization is just getting started my immediate future remains somewhat of a mystery. The outfit will have a "public interest" orientation, and will be examining issues on both the domestic and international scene which seem to merit more public (and, of course, political) attention than they have been getting.' Roger reports that he spent the spring term as Visiting Professor of International Relations at Johns Hopkins, and that 'my book, *The Politics of Mexican Development*, appeared six months late—May 1, 1971—and very overpriced—$11.00. Nevertheless, it has what my Managing Editor calls a "gorgeous cover," so buy it.' "

"I formed very early the suspicion that he was working for the CIA, which I'm sure a lot of other people had as well," I was told by Dick Pfaff, who is now a professor of history at the University of North Carolina and also an Episcopalian priest. "And I have no grounds for saying this except the very cloaked language he would use about these improbably titled jobs he had." Potomac Associates does sound like a CIA front, but apparently there was nothing more sinister about it than the suspicion that it might prove to be a source of position papers for the presidential campaign of John V. Lindsay—a suspicion that, according to its director, proved to be unfounded. "No word from HANSEN again this year," the secretary wrote in 1974, "but your secretary can report indirectly that the pervasive seepage from the Watergate spread even to Roger this year. It would appear that among the many memos which have 'come to light' this year was one outlining plans, apparently never executed, for the 'Plumbers' to 'penetrate' an outfit called Potomac Associates. While driving from Los Angeles to La Jolla one day last winter, I was treated to a CBS radio interview with the Director of Potomac Associates at the time of contemplated 'penetration.' I can well recall the total and complete bewilderment with which the Director, who, of course, was none other than Roger Hansen, wondered aloud what on earth the Plumbers could have been after."

In 1977, Denny was heard from again. "HANSEN sent a prompt reply to my plea for news, as he was on the eve of a trip to the Far East in his capacity as a Senior Staff Member of the National Security Council. In September, he will 'retire' to become Jacob Blaustein Professor of International Organization at the Johns Hopkins School of Advanced International Studies in Washington. He was hoping to finish by December a book for the Council on Foreign Relations' '1980s Project.' The subject is the evolving relations between the developed and developing nations." Then, having announced a move to the institution he was to be with for the rest of his life, Denny disappeared from the Class of 1957 class letter. As far as I can tell, his name didn't appear again until the spring of 1991, when the secretary—by then Don Smith, the Grinnell historian —wrote, "While preparing this letter, I received the sad news of Roger HANSEN's death by suicide early in the year. 'Denny' had two ebullient years at Magdalen, and those who knew him there will be grateful for those years and for his warm-hearted friendship."

14

FOR those who had gathered the evening of the memorial service in Tersh Boasberg's living room—even those who agreed with Rocky Suddarth that Denny had been in trouble from the start—analyzing Denny's life seemed to be partly a matter of trying to isolate the moment when, as a couple of people had put it, he began to lose his direction. Most of the people in the room had themselves been highly directed since grade school. They were not just Denny people, they were fifties people—fifties high achievers, mainly, who had grown up thinking that the life of a fifties golden boy had the smooth trajectory of an airliner rising from the ground. If things didn't work out that way, it's natural for them to look for the moment when the motor started sputtering.

Somebody at Tersh's had said that the problem facing people who breeze through high school and college the way Denny did is that they get no training in losing, so the first defeat can be devastating. Denny did have some training—for instance, he had apparently been deeply disappointed that his performance as a swimmer at Yale did not match the record-breaking swimming he had done for the Sequoia Cherokees—but he also had the awful insecurity that had been present even when he seemed to be a person who could lose at nothing. George E. Vaillant's longitudinal study of members of a Harvard class twenty years ahead of us begins with the proposition that mental health is measured in how well someone adapts to the setbacks that are bound to occur; the book is called *Adaptation to Life*. There are those who believe that at some point Denny was unable to adapt because, as one of them put it, "something happened and he decided his life was worthless." The stories of failed golden boys all of us heard just after Denny died tended to have such moments—the career path mistake, the panic that cost the golden boy his confidence. For some of the people who interpret Denny's life that way, Oxford was the moment.

It seems clear that Denny had been concerned about the possibility that Oxford would be the place where he would be revealed at last as unworthy of his glories. When I spoke to Howard Lamar about Denny, he said, "I think the Rhodes Scholarship produced a great deal of worry: 'I have handled this subculture. Can I handle another one?'" As the 1957 Rhodes Scholars sailed to Southampton from New York—they all went over together, through an arrangement with the United States Lines—it was assumed that all of them had read a piece in *Life* called "A Farewell to Bright College Years?" That must have swollen the trepidation Denny would have already been feeling. The followup piece that *Life* did on Denny two or three months after he arrived at Oxford—a short picture spread headlined MAN OF ELI AT OXFORD—was hardly reassuring. One sentence says, "Surrounded by British undergraduates whose erudition often staggers him, Hansen could not keep up with their practice of reading books in French and German, and had to ask his tutor to assign books only in English."

After mentioning Denny's complaints about the accommodations and the food, the piece does say that "Hansen is happily getting into the spirit of Oxford life." The pictures and captions, though, are not happy. The full-page shot that opens the piece is the picture of Denny riding his bicycle on the sidewalk. Seeing that picture brought back memories of listening to Denny's complaints—we were in a café in London, if I remember correctly—about the perfidy of the *Life* crew in setting up a shot that made him look like a hick who didn't even know that bicycles were for the street. One of the pictures shows Denny pouring tea into some cups arrayed on the floor of his room while some other Americans, smiling self-consciously, watch him with great care, as if observing a mildly antic science experiment. "He had learned how to make tea only the day before," the caption says. The other picture of Denny's attempt to acclimate shows him playing darts at a pub, and notes that while the other American students drank mild and bitter ("a mixture of light and dark ale") Hansen had orangeade. The picture that outraged him almost as much as the bicycle shot shows him sitting in a chair with a blanket across his lap. "Muffled against cold in his damp rooms in Magdalen College," it says, "Hansen does his studying sustained by Ovaltine and bread filched from dining hall." Not just a boob and a prig, as Denny read it, but also a petty thief.

When that follow-up piece came out in *Life*, I was working at Time Inc. in London, in a temporary job that had emerged accidentally from a summer job as I was about to leave for Europe to wait for the draft. I could hardly have been further from the center of the company's editorial power. I spent a lot of my time answering queries from the researchers of various Time Inc. magazines in New York—queries that all seemed to begin "Need soonest," in the pigeon cable-ese then favored for communication over the leased wire, and all seemed to ask for information that nobody could possibly ever need soonest or any other time. (My favorite one read—in its entirety, as I remember—"*Fortune* needs soonest name of longest street in London uninterrupted by intersections.") But I was the target of opportunity for any complaints Denny had about how he had been treated by *Life.* I tried to respond the way any jaded reporter would have responded; I had, after all, been in the game a good three weeks. I probably told him it was routine for someone portrayed in a magazine to be sensitive about little things that readers wouldn't even notice—especially someone dumb enough to pose riding a bicycle on the sidewalk. Rereading the piece after Denny's death, though, I had to admit that, particularly compared with the "*Life* Goes to a Commencement" tone of the original article, there was something snide about it. I also realized that it may have represented the first time that adults had commented on his activities in terms that were anything but completely glowing. It may have been, in Denny's view, the first time someone had managed to see what was under the mask.

I also realized, after talking about Denny with some of

the other people who were Rhodes Scholars at the time, that the *Life* reporter who had visited Denny at Oxford was, if not absolutely prescient, at least closer to the truth than Denny realized at the time. When Robert Tucker and I spoke, not long after the memorial service, about what he called Denny's sense of "not being up to things," he said, "My feeling is that this was enormously exacerbated at Oxford. He worked under people like A.J.P. Taylor— that's enough to give you an inferiority complex. They'd say, 'This is a good effort. Not top drawer, of course.' I think at Oxford it became blindingly clear that there were levels that he couldn't attain. A lot of Rhodes Scholars have suffered this reaction to Oxford." Other Rhodes Scholars tend to remember Denny as a sort of loner at Oxford—someone who didn't make a lot of friends, particularly among the English. In those days, there were always Americans at Oxford who took on English airs— people who carried tightly rolled umbrellas at all times and got fussy about their scones and began using enough English slang and English inflection to blur the American in their speech. Denny, everyone agrees, was not one of them. He may have learned to make tea and to order brown and bitter, but he remained an unreconstructed American. "He was sort of a California sunshine kid," Dick Pfaff, who was in Magdalen College with Denny and also read history, told me. "There was a lot of gee-whizzery about him." He didn't hang around with the intellectual set. Unlike a lot of Rhodes Scholars, he didn't compete for his college in sports. "Oxford was a downer for Denny," Joe Clayton wrote in his letter to Don Smith. "He had no captive audience in a community of prima donnas and he was too far from the California sun. Thereafter, he just couldn't seem to get it together."

But Smith had said "two ebullient years at Magdalen," and when I spoke to him he seemed to remember someone who was closer to the Denny of Yale—someone who still had that sense of discovery, about opera, for instance, and travel. "I think in some ways maybe I feel kind of lucky to know him when I did," Smith, who was a close friend of Denny's during their second year at Oxford, told me not long after Denny's death. "That is, maybe if I had been a student with him at Yale I would have seen the kind of icon, the golden boy from California. Later on, if he became morose and difficult, if you had gotten to know him then it might have been 'Hey, what's the big deal about this guy?' But in the second year at Oxford, I saw the sort of charm and the appeal and the good humor, but I saw this extraordinarily appealing kind of vulnerability. Which in some ways was gratifying for a kid from Tennessee who had never been out of the South until I went over there. I sort of fell in love with operatic music and so on, and here was this guy who liked the same things." Also, the notion that Oxford is where Denny confirmed his fears of not being able to measure up to the next challenge are contradicted by his academic performance. Rhodes Scholars rarely get Firsts—there were only four in the Class of 1957—but apparently Denny, despite having fallen so ill that he had to take his oral examination in the hospital, barely missed one. In an obituary of Denny written for *The American Oxonian*, Van Ooms, a Rhodes Scholar one year earlier, quoted a friend of Denny's who said, "Who knows what might have happened had he been sitting up?"

Years later, I found out that Howard Lamar had been concerned by the tone of Denny's letters from Oxford. "He was very much the visitor, the observer," Lamar told me. "They were not written as a participant. They were letters from someone on a trip." In fact, Lamar told me during that conversation, five undergraduates he had known well had become Rhodes Scholars, and he thought three had been badly damaged by the experience—partly because of becoming ensnared in a British academic culture that makes it hard to fit in back in the United States, partly because of the burden of expectations they had to carry. Don Smith believes that the burden of expectations is a problem for almost all Rhodes Scholars, and particularly Denny, because of the *Life* articles. "I have vivid memories of saying once to a friend, 'The worst thing that ever happened to me was getting the Rhodes Scholarship' or 'If I hadn't gotten the Rhodes Scholarship I wouldn't have had some of the advantages but maybe things would have been easier for me,' " he told me. "It would be very surprising to me if the ordinary recipient of the Rhodes had not had thoughts like that at one time or the other." Smith hadn't seen Denny for many years before Denny's death; he had been conscious of Denny's distancing himself from his Oxford friends even in the seventies. But when Denny died, Smith said, "I thought, Oh my God, what if I was, in a sense, the problem? What if I was one of these people he thought he was accountable to—one of those people in Oxford who was some kind of judge . . . Because he didn't have anything to live up to as far as I was concerned except to be himself."

15

I last saw Denny as an Oxford student when he came through Paris on the spring vacation of his first year. I had moved to the *Time* bureau in Paris, the original agreement having been that I would spend two months there after four months in London. A month or so later, as the Fourth Republic began to collapse under pressure from the war in Algeria, I was sent to Tunisia, so that *Time* would have somebody there—even somebody who hadn't been absolutely clear about where Tunisia was—to make a phone call if the French military invaded in pursuit of Algerian guerrillas. (After being in the company of a gaggle of British foreign correspondents for the first time, I wrote friends in England to say that I had been hasty a couple of months before when I said that *Scoop* was, although hilariously funny, a bit broad.) I traveled in Europe for a few months, and by the time Denny started his second year at Oxford I was back in the States. I could sympathize with what Pudge had called Denny's "indecision about his career path." I was carrying the rallying cry of people our age—"I'm not sure what I want to do"—to its logical extreme: I didn't exactly want to do anything.

Even though I knew that people changed courses of study and jobs and even entire careers all the time, I couldn't shake the notion that once you started on one path or the other, you were stuck with it. When I got out of college, I didn't know what I wanted to do, and the one thing I was clear about not wanting to do was to start being a grownup. Years later, I happened to read an article that described the frame of mind I had been in and referred to it as Provisional Life Syndrome—an unwillingness to start adult life. I'm sure that was not what my father called it. Concerned by my lack of focus—looking back, I realize he must have thought that the entire Grand Plan was in danger of collapsing just as the first stage was successfully completed—he had decided that I should go to law school, and think about returning to Kansas City to take a position with a law firm he had in mind. "You used to think I was going to be President," I finally told him. "Now you think I should come back home and advise somebody on the tax implications of his real estate deal? This is quite a comedown." President? Yes, my father believed that any American boy could grow up to be President, and I was, of course, the nearest American boy at hand.

Fortunately for me, the presidential part of the plan had become a sort of family joke by the time I was in high school. Whatever the ultimate goal, I didn't want to go to law school. I had left for Europe, ignoring suggestions that I should take advantage of the new reserve training law that allowed you to satisfy your military obligation by going into a reserve or National Guard unit for six months and then going to any weekly meetings you couldn't concoct a way to get out of. Eventually, I was drafted. When Denny entered the Woodrow Wilson School at Princeton, two years after we got out of Yale, I was a soldier stationed on Governors Island, in New York Harbor, with another year in the Army ahead of me. If a bunch of Ivy League high achievers had gathered in a living room thirty years later to analyze my life, I suspect they would have identified that period as the moment I began to lose my direction. At the time, I might have had some feelings along those lines myself.

I must have seen Denny occasionally in New York during that period—I found a letter to my parents mentioning that I had met his boat when he returned from England—but I have a strong memory of only one meeting, at Princeton. I drove over from Fort Dix, New Jersey, where I was on temporary duty for a day or two as the driver for a major from our office on Governors Island—the public information office for First U.S. Army headquarters—who thought he ought to be on hand to make certain that the mustering out of Elvis Presley went off without a hitch. Although Elvis was the symbol of rebellion, the entertainer who many thought could not appear on the *Ed Sullivan Show* because of his lewd gyrations, his manager had decided that it would be a good career move for him to report cheerfully for the draft and serve two years in an Army line unit with ordinary draftees—a reflection of how far rebellion went in the late fifties. The Elvis mustering out was not my only brush with the celebrated during my Army career. When General Douglas MacArthur, long retired from active duty, had a prostate operation at Lenox Hill

Hospital, I was part of a group assigned to work out of a room down the hall writing releases on how many pats of butter and soft-boiled eggs he had consumed each day during his recuperation—a military operation we referred to as the "wee-wee patrol." When Nikita Khrushchev, on his first trip to the United States, arrived in New York by train from Washington and turned to wave out the window to the waiting throngs, he found only me—a solitary figure on an adjoining platform, dressed in the uniform of an Army private, holding the bull mike I had just used to inform the press traveling on another train which stairway to take. I waved back.

I remember sitting in the back booth of a coffee shop in Princeton with Denny—joking, gossiping, analyzing the phenomenon of Elvis Presley, speculating as to the nature of the machinations that had resulted in Nancy Sinatra's being present to welcome Elvis to civilian life. I might have told Denny that those of us who were counting on a role in his Administration were not thrilled about the extension of his academic life, but I never got a specific answer to the question Denny's college friends had been asking: What in the hell was he doing at the Woodrow Wilson School of Public and International Affairs? What was the point of getting an additional master's degree? Why wasn't he in law school? Why wasn't he in California running for the state legislature? Why did Denny seem to be more or less parked when he was supposed to be out there getting on with it?

There was something about Denny's time at Princeton reminiscent of a diver shifting from foot to foot on the board but unwilling to make the dive. Among the faculty, he apparently had a reputation as an exceedingly capable and often charming young man—brilliant, some said—who wasn't working up to his capacities. His marks were considerably below his usual standards. "He has in many ways a brilliant mind," one member of the faculty wrote in a letter that had to do with the possibility of a job offer. "Hansen is a man of very considerable ability, of which he was perhaps overly aware. His one fault here seemed to us to be that he wanted to 'start at the top.' " Having been unsuccessful in his effort to get into the Foreign Service—in a letter at the time, he said that the problem was his bad back—he seemed, at least to one professor, to lack "a sense of urgency in facing the world and his place in it."

Denny's time at Princeton could be seen as bolstering a theory I heard from one of the people who knew him at Oxford and ran into him while he was at the Woodrow Wilson School: "I thought that because of some private sorrow, he was not going to push himself beyond what he needed to do." Except that he continued to push himself. He was as interested in perfection when he worked for Ted Geiger at the National Planning Association as he had been as a swimmer for the Sequoia Cherokees. He was still called Denny when he left Princeton, and apparently arrived in Washington as the same Denny who had so impressed my father at commencement weekend—in the words of Bob Semple, a friend of mine from the *Yale Daily News* who became a friend of Denny's in Washington, "an all-purpose boy hero." As Semple remembers him from those early days in Washington, Denny was "totally fresh, full of beans, intelligent, a good listener. Vital! And he had that smile!"

16

AFTER Denny joined the staff of Senator Harrison Williams, of New Jersey, I let him know now and then how fascinating I thought it must be to come to grips with the more serious issues of, say, urban mass transit and Title II housing. But I think working on the staff of a well-regarded senator struck most people as an appropriate start-out job for an all-purpose boy hero. I saw Denny in Washington from time to time during those early days of the sixties, when the Kennedy Administration was getting under way and Washington seemed to be entering an era ready-made for bright young men from the Ivy League. I remember being at a farewell party in the Georgetown house Denny shared, for someone in the group—it must have been Rocky Suddarth—who was about to embark for his first Foreign Service posting, in Bomoko, Mali. The songs being sung had lines like "You be my Bomoko baby, I'll be your Mali dolly." The group of people Denny lived with in Georgetown changed steadily, but just about everyone in it could be described without qualification as a bright young man from the Ivy League, prepared to step into a grown-up version of the "youthful meritocracy."

John Poole, who graduated from Harvard the year before we got out of Yale, was one of the young men in the Georgetown arrangement and one of the people who was at Tersh's that evening. He now works for the antitrust division of the Justice Department. "There was an assumption of rising in the government or industry," he recalled, when we met in Washington to speak about that era. "You did feel like a most favored person in those days, particularly if you had been at places like Harvard and Yale. We were the brightest of the richest and most powerful country. We had the feeling our parents had sacrificed a bit and that we had certain obligations. But you also felt that whatever you wanted to do you could do it. I remember the evening when Dick Brady, who was just starting at Covington & Burling, came back late from the firm dinner while a game of Diplomacy was going on. He was in black tie, and he was accompanied by Dean Acheson, who of course said something about having played a certain amount of that game himself."

The people in Denny's crowd weren't old enough to know Kennedy. They knew people who worked for him. Probably the only person Denny saw regularly in Washington who was at a level of government beyond the first posting was James C. Thomson, Jr., who was working for the State Department. Jim Thomson had graduated from Yale just before we arrived, but he had met Denny later at Keys; they became better acquainted when Denny arrived in Washington, wearing, in Thomson's words, "a shiny California face and the Howard Lamar imprimatur." Thomson, who grew up in China, had been a sort of golden boy at Yale himself—someone who expounded fully formed positions on foreign affairs as chairman of the *Yale Daily News*. His wife, Diana, remembers being at a Washington dinner party in the early sixties at which every male present took it for granted that he was part of the meritocracy that would one day run the country. "Oh, you men!" she said. "You all want to be President." She meant it literally, except, of course, that she knew very well that one of the men present was expected to become Secretary of State instead. Thirty years later, when George Bush was defeated by Bill Clinton and much was written about how the generation that had fought the Second World War had finally handed over the reins to the baby-boom generation, I could imagine the men who had been at that dinner party, members of the generation in between, thinking, Hey, you skipped us!

By the standards I had in the early sixties—I was working for *Time* in New York and living in an apartment in the Village that, after a couple of years of habitation, still regularly drew the comment "You could do wonders with this"—the Georgetown group led a pretty fancy life. A woman came in a couple of times a week to cook dinner. There were parties that were almost in the nature of soirées. Occasionally, there would be a waltz evening: the furniture would be cleared, the floor waxed, a considerable supply of cheap German white wine laid in, and the guests would show up in formal dress. There were parties in the garden. Among the people who showed up regularly were Bob Semple, who had gone from graduate work at Berkeley to a Dow Jones paper called *The National Observer*, and his then wife, Susan Semple—the former Sue Kirk, Denny's date in the pages of *Life*. "In a way, it was more like a grown-up married style of living than our life," Bob Semple has recalled. "John Poole and Denny were very fastidious. They served hors d'oeuvres. They selected wines, although I can't imagine what wines were made that we knew about. Meanwhile, we'd have old-fashioned college arguments and light chitchat, like whether McGeorge Bundy was worth a shit. We were in our middle and late twenties, and we tried to redesign the world verbally. I thought these guys would run the country someday. In a way, it was a wonderful moment. Somehow, we paid the bills, hung out, had enough booze. And we could get up early the next morning and go to work. Everyone seemed to have an unlimited future. You couldn't beat it. It was the growing up that was the difficulty."

"When he was on," John Poole says of Denny, "he seemed to be someone who shared your view of the world. He was funny. He was absolutely honest." Sometimes he wasn't on, and Poole remembers wondering every day whether it was going to be one of Denny's good mornings or bad mornings. Denny was having some aches and pains—including a case of what seemed to be the gout, a disease so rare in an otherwise healthy, athletic twenty-five-year-old man that for a while the National Institutes of Health kept an eye on him. It turned out not to be the gout, but I only learned that years later. At the time, it was something else to kid him about. When I heard about his condition, I wrote him a one-line letter. I don't think I even bothered to sign it; the *Time* stationery would have told the tale. It said, "Think old, get the gout." When I talk with people who saw a lot of Denny in those days, it strikes me that women tended to have a less sunny view of him than men did. That seemed to be the case with Jim and Diana Thomson and also with Warren and Teeny Zimmerman, another married couple with close friends in the Georgetown group. Warren Zimmerman, who was then starting out in the State Department and eventually became Ambassador to Yugoslavia, remembers that era as a time when "everyone had it made, and Denny seemed to have it made better than anyone." Teeny Zimmerman remembers Denny as a man who was palpably sad.

Denny was close to the Semples in the early sixties, and he remained close until Bob, who had moved from *The National Observer* to *The New York Times*, was transferred to New York. For several years, Denny and Carol Austin would go to the Semples' for Christmas dinner. He was the old charming Denny at dinner. Carol Austin says that after what was often a grumpy ride over to the Semples' house in Cleveland Park, she could see him rev up his group personality as they stood outside the front door. But at some point, Semple told me, "he had these conversations with Susan and me: 'Jesus, I'm twenty-five years old and I'm a Senate aide.' We'd have these long discussions. Essentially, he was asking two friends: What should I be doing? Then, all of a sudden, something didn't work out somewhere and he said he was going to Cleveland to work in television. That was, I think, the moment. I think we both thought, Uh-oh. The guy's at sea. He had lost his bearings in this quest for a career that by all rights should have come out of Yale and the Rhodes Scholarship. I thought, The guy's lost it, and it's too early to lose it."

Of course, it's common for people in their twenties to have crises of confidence. It's common for people in their twenties to worry about whether they're in the right field after all. Someone familiar with attendance patterns at Yale class reunions once told me that attendance drops appreciably from the tenth reunion, which normally draws a large crowd, to the fifteenth. There are, of course, a number of theories to explain that—including the theory that physical deterioration, particularly among males, seems to accelerate in one's early and middle thirties. The theory favored by my informant, though, was that by the time the fifteenth reunion comes around—the graduates are now, say, thirty-six or thirty-seven—someone is pretty set in the sort of career he's going to have. He's in his slot, and it may be apparent how far he has or hasn't moved in it. It is too late to show up as a promising young man who has not quite found himself. It is too late to say casually over a drink that you might decide to go to law school after all.

Bob Semple and I stuck to the field we were in when we were in our twenties—he is on the editorial board of the *Times*—but I can't say that the possibility of going to law school was never mentioned. When I'm asked about journalism as a career, I often mention a conversation Semple and I once had in Washington when he was still working for *The National Observer*—a paper I remember mainly for a self-conscious folksiness that resulted in a lot of quotes that began something like "Folks around here reckon . . ." This was in 1963, when I stopped in Washington on my way to Georgia. A couple of years before, I had spent a year in the South as a reporter for *Time*, and I was going back to do my first article for *The New Yorker*—a piece about the two black students who had desegregated the University of Georgia while I was covering such events for *Time* and who were now about to graduate. Semple and I were standing on the sidewalk in front of the Jefferson Hotel. He told me a story. He said that one day he had arrived back in the office after covering a particularly boring and senseless hearing. He was trying, unsuccessfully, to get somebody on the telephone so that person could lie to him about the subject of the hearing. He glanced around at other people in the newsroom who were trying to get people on the telephone for similar purposes. Suddenly a question floated into his mind: "Is this a job for a college graduate?"

The short answer, of course, is not necessarily. There's a lot of grunt work to it—a lot of sitting in outer offices, a lot of getting lost in bad neighborhoods, a lot of wrestling with sentences that will probably not be noticed by anybody else—and as far as I know, nobody has ever figured out a way to separate the grunt work from the sort of work for which Semple's impressive education might prove useful. Denny actually had three or four jobs in television journalism—all held briefly. One of his first jobs out of Princeton was to work for Robert Abernathy as a sort of researcher for an afternoon program on NBC geared to high-school students—a job that, in Abernathy's recollection, he did with extraordinary competence and enthusiasm until the show went off the air. He was a writer for NBC News in Washington for a while. The job he left the night he was supposed to have dinner with me in 1964 was at NBC; as Carol Austin heard the story, he assured his exit by calling his boss—the man who hired him in order to be reported to by four people—a horse's ass. Being a local TV reporter in Cleveland sounds like the least likely of his television jobs, and from what he told Carol Austin and others, he disliked it the most.

"He simply hated it," she told me. "He considered it degrading to stand around a corridor and then shove a microphone into someone's face." Denny was in Cleveland for less than a year. John Dancey, who is now NBC's State Department reporter, was at the station at the time, and he remembers Denny as a good writer who was trying to learn the skills of broadcasting—someone who was "closed in" and had to work to be a public person. One other thing he remembers about Denny, Dancey told me, was that "he was better educated than anyone else in the newsroom." The station manager who hired Denny, Pat Trese, eventually concluded that he was an unhappy young man. "He lacked a certain social skill," Trese told me. "You can take some people and plop them down anywhere and they'll thrive. A lot of guys on the staff were like that. There was something about his air—kind of Ivy League. I don't mean that he was too big for his britches. He wasn't like that. I had the feeling that it was not the right place for him. Maybe there wasn't any right place for him."

Lacked a certain social skill? Closed in? Ivy League air? Could this be Denny Hansen, who attracted a coterie when he was plopped down on the Old Campus of Yale from Sequoia Union High School? Where was the Denny Hansen who wowed everybody's parents at graduation—the person who acted completely natural while he was being photographed the entire weekend by Alfred Eisenstaedt?

Where was the Denny Hansen who, even in the early days in Washington, had, in Susan Semple's words, "the ability to make people feel comfortable, the ability to make people feel as intelligent as he was"?

I suspect that some of the people at the "Big Chill" session might have said that the impression Denny made on his colleagues in Cleveland—as well as the impression he gave at Princeton of expecting to "start at the top"— reflected a problem in making the adjustment that college golden boys have to make as they enter a world in which, as Bob Semple once put it, "the newsroom is full of guys just as smart as you are." I couldn't help wondering whether all this might have had something to do with the style that held sway at Yale in the fifties, which may have left us with some reluctance to be caught striving. Was one of the things Denny (and the rest of us) had picked up at Yale a tone that we would have considered cool and others might see as an Ivy League air? Had Yale taken someone who had been an unambiguous hero—someone who was to high-school students what Frank Sinatra was to popular music—and given him a crippling disdain for anything that smacked of wearing your letter sweater with the letter showing? Maybe. But Denny's demeanor in Cleveland indicated more serious problems than that. The person described to me by people who had worked at that television station didn't sound like Denny. He sounded more like Roger.

17

AT around the time Denny stood me up for dinner, in
1964, we both started the grown-up life we had spent
a few years in the late fifties putting off—the life that puts
you in the slot you're going to be in when you appear (or,
more likely, don't appear) at the fifteenth reunion. Covering the civil rights story in the South for *Time* had been
my first serious job. It was a long way from the vibrations
of power that excited some of the residents of Denny's
house in Georgetown—two of the expense account items
I remember were "Pants ruined in racial disturbance—
$25.00" and "After-prayer-meeting snack, Tuskegee—
$3.75"—but it excited me. Even though it occurred to me
that an aversion to calling strangers on the telephone was
a slight handicap to a reporter, I was probably hooked. By
1964, I had published the University of Georgia piece as
a three-part series in *The New Yorker* and as a book. I
took it for granted that, whether reporting was a job for
a college graduate or not, it was the sort of job I was going
to have. I had met the woman I was going to marry. My
life was no longer provisional.

That came about, of course, partly by pure chance—an element we underrated in 1957 when we thought about our futures. By chance, for instance, there was an opening at the *Time* bureau in Atlanta when I got out of the Army. By chance, the civil rights story, which had sometimes been becalmed for a year or two at a time, erupted the year I spent in the South in a way that was bound to engage anyone vaguely interested in reporting—sit-in movements, the Freedom Rides, the desegregation of the University of Georgia and the public schools of New Orleans and Atlanta. It was also by chance—during that fall of 1964, around the time Lyndon B. Johnson managed to defeat Barry Goldwater without using so much as a paragraph of the speeches I had written for him, and the country had thus been saved, I figured, from someone who was perfectly capable of sending American boys to Southeast Asia—that Denny walked into Ted Geiger's office at the National Planning Association and began, whether he realized it or not, to ease himself into his slot.

The National Planning Association had come into being during the Second World War, when a group of economists and business executives and labor leaders decided that some planning ought to be done as to how the economy was going to be converted back to peacetime needs once the war ended. It evolved into a place that did long-term studies—one of which led to the act that established the Council of Economic Advisers. By the time Denny showed up, Geiger, a former foreign service officer who had worked with the Marshall Plan, was running an operation with a budget of about a million and a half dollars a year and was looking for an assistant. He was bowled over by

Denny. The job interview went on for a few hours. Denny and Ted Geiger seemed to have the same view of history, the same notion of who was worth reading and who wasn't. In Geiger's words, "We were two people reading from the same hymnbook." Denny signed on with Geiger and enrolled at the Johns Hopkins School of Advanced International Studies so he could work toward his doctorate at the same time.

SAIS was not ordinarily thought of as a place to work on a doctorate. It was, and is, overwhelmingly a school for people who need a master's degree. In general, its faculty, then and now, concentrates on the professional and policy side of international affairs rather than on the theoretical side. For someone who has an academic career in mind, the doctoral degree SAIS does award, a Ph.D. in international relations, doesn't fit in well with the way conventional universities are organized, since hiring is ordinarily by departments that fill positions in, say, history or economics or political science. For Denny's purposes, though, SAIS had the overwhelming advantage of being only a couple of blocks from the National Planning Association. The connection between his job and his studies turned out to go beyond just physical proximity. As Geiger reminded me, Asia and Africa and Latin America had been more or less rediscovered in the fifties as places where the United States had an interest in economic development, and by the mid-sixties there was already some disenchantment about the pace of the efforts. The NPA was funded to do four or five case studies of progress that had been made, and Geiger assigned Denny to do the one on Mexico. Denny managed to piggyback his doctoral work onto the study, and the result was the thesis that became his book *The Politics of Mexican Development*.

According to everyone in the field I spoke to after Denny's death, *The Politics of Mexican Development* was a brilliant book—a study that brought in political and social and historical elements to analyze Mexican economic development in a completely fresh way. When it was published, in 1971, it was widely reviewed, including a large review (coupled with a book on Cuba) in *The New York Times Book Review*. The reviewer in *The American Political Science Review* wrote, "Roger Hansen has written a book that no serious scholar of Mexico or the Latin American scene can afford to ignore," and despite all that has happened since in the field of Mexican development, that is apparently still true: the book has never gone out of print. Its success, I assume, was partly what propelled Denny toward a specialty in the politics of international economic relations, particularly the relations between the industrialized countries and what people in the field call LDCs, or Less Developed Countries—a complicated jumble of economics and politics that came to be known as the North-South Agenda. Mainly as a fellow of the Overseas Development Council, he was prominent in outlining what he called a constructive American response to the demands of the LDCs that the prevailing pattern of trade and investment and foreign assistance be changed in a way that would accelerate economic growth in the countries roughly grouped under the category of the South. As Riordan Roett had said at Denny's memorial service, Denny's work "set the agenda" for consideration of North-South issues. In other words, my impression in those days that Denny was doing quite well, even if it happened to be in the sort of endeavor that did not ordinarily lead to the White House, was not far off.

He had his problems, of course. When he entered analysis, in the sixties, he had told Ted Geiger that he was doing it for three reasons: because he wasn't able to deal with authority, because he had unreasonably high standards and punished himself for falling short of them, and because if he didn't get some help he might end up as a homosexual. The analysis, Geiger had said at Tersh's, hadn't removed any of Denny's problems ("All that it did was make him understand whatever they were better. And he was in that very, very unhappy state in which he knew: he could observe himself. He could see everything that he did that antagonized people, that made him difficult. But he couldn't control himself. He had no control over his feelings, over his inner conflict. And that led to a turning in of the anger against himself for his failure to do things"). His relationships with those in authority were still marked by sudden explosions and vituperative letters. On the project the Council on Foreign Relations was doing on the eighties, for instance, he struck up friendships with some of his colleagues, like Catherine Gwin ("He had to be coddled, but he was fabulously fun to work with intellectually") and Edward Morse, who thought of Denny as a person of great quality and humor ("neurotic, but no more than most people I've known"). But the director of the project, Richard Ullman, saw Denny as someone who, aside from the occasional explosions, spent a lot of time complaining about his health and his personal problems, and didn't always pull his load. Looking back, Ullman—who was a Rhodes Scholar in 1956 and is now at the Woodrow Wilson School—summed up Denny's participation in the project from a boss's point of view with one sentence: "He was impossible to work with."

The personal problem of Denny's that people on the 1980s Project heard the most about was his split up with Carol Austin, in 1975. Denny's feelings for Carol Austin seemed to involve much more than his interest in her as some sort of cover, although that element must have been present. After his death, the precise nature of their relationship wasn't a matter I found myself eager to explore. That sort of thing has never been my reporting specialty, even while poking around in the lives of strangers, and I was aware that I was delving into areas that Denny and I, two sons of the fifties, would have probably never discussed in person. I did have a couple of long visits with Carol, who shared her memories of Denny as someone both special and maddening—a sometimes charming and brilliant man who could fly into a serious rage over his failure to get the storm windows on.

She said that their relationship had turned out to be more of a friendship than a romance, even though he often spoke of marriage and his friends treated them as a couple. In those years, she said, she thought of him not as someone who might be gay but as someone who, for reasons some psychiatrist was busy trying to dredge up, shrank from affectionate human contact of any sort. The second- or third-hand snippets I got of his view of things made their relationship sound a bit like one of those long, soulful, agonizingly chaste romances in the fifties that were supposed to end up in marriage if neither party perished of exhaustion along the way—except that those involved people in their late teens and didn't last ten years. I suppose you could argue that Denny hung on to the possibility of marrying Carol Austin as his chance to live what we had all been brought up to think of as a normal life. I don't know that. I do know that he was terribly upset when they parted, and terribly upset again when she, six or seven years later, married someone else.

Still, as Ted Geiger put it, "in the seventies he was functional." In 1973, for instance, when there was a search for a position in the political science department at Swarthmore, Denny made a very favorable impression, and apparently finished second to a strong internal candidate. There were two overlapping but not identical communities in Washington—a foreign policy community and a development community—and for a while Denny ("one of the people who put the North-South Agenda on the map") moved in both of them. He was even taken up by one or two Washington hostesses, and according to Carol Austin, he found that rather satisfying. Whatever his problems at the 1980s Project, the book that emerged from his efforts was considered first-rate. Around that time, Peter Krogh, who was already the dean of the School of Foreign Service at Georgetown, started a small group called the Society, made up of some contemporaries around Washington who were, whatever their political beliefs, concerned that after Vietnam and the Watergate scandal the United States might be tempted to retreat into isolationism. "The notion was definitely there that these people were in positions of responsibility and likely to be in positions of more responsibility, and should be in contact with one another," Krogh told me. In other words, they were people of promise, and among them was Roger D. Hansen.

18

———

RIGHT at that moment—in June of 1976, when he was moving in rather sophisticated circles in Washington and was apparently known to some people in the field as "Mr. North-South" and was, as it turned out, a good bet for a post in the White House if Jimmy Carter won the election—Denny passed up the opportunity to return to California for the twenty-fifth reunion of the Sequoia High School Class of 1953. It had, of course, been only twenty-three years since the Class of 1953 graduated. I discussed the unusual timing with Carolyn Krogh—Peter Krogh's sister, who graduated from Sequoia with Denny. Carolyn, whose father was the principal of the school at the time she and Peter and Denny were there, lives an hour or so away from Redwood City now, and she turned out to be one of the people in the class who organizes reunions and tries to keep track of far-flung classmates. She worked on not only the twenty-fifth—or twenty-third—but also the thirty-fifth, which Denny also skipped. Carolyn told me that in 1976 one member of the class, Mike Gavin, happened to have an assignment from NBC to write and produce and direct a documentary that would compare a high-school class graduating that June with a class that had graduated from the same school a generation before. Logically, the comparison would have been with a class gathered for its twenty-fifth reunion as the Class of 1976 graduated, but Gavin presumably decided to trade symmetry for familiarity with the cast of characters: NBC told Gavin's class that it would underwrite the twenty-fifth reunion if the class was willing to have it two years early, and the film credits say forthrightly, "NBC organized the Class of 1953 reunion for filming purposes."

The film opens against the background music of the Sequoia High School alma mater: "Sequoia, Sequoia—friendly, dear Sequoia. We, thy children, voices raise. Voices raise in the praise. Beautiful, beautiful Sequoia." There are shots of a campus that is indeed beautiful—although not as beautiful as it once was, the commentary informs us, since the changing sexual mores of teenagers over the years made keeping students out of the bushes so difficult that it was finally decided simply to remove some of the bushes. There are shots of the returning Class of 1953, kidding around or dancing to songs like "They Tried to Tell Us We're Too Young"—shots that reminded me of my own twenty-fifth high-school reunion in Kansas City, a warm and jokey occasion symbolized for me by the memory of Chuck McDaneld wearing Carol Jean Hall's name badge all weekend.

For our twenty-fifth, Eddie Williams—my childhood friend who had gone to Princeton with Eberhard Faber the Pencil King—had decided that he and I had to design a survey of the class, dealing partly with how our classmates thought the world had treated them since graduation. Eddie—who was, and is, teaching Spanish literature at San Francisco State—expressed concern from the start about whether we could get a straight answer out of the people we had been to high school with, many of whom shared Chuck McDaneld's sense of humor. That concern seemed well placed as the surveys began to arrive. We had designed an elaborate process for the preservation of anonymity, but Eddie phoned from San Francisco to say that the first form returned said in huge Magic Marker letters whose survey it was. It had occurred to Eddie that one of our classmates might have put someone else's name on his own survey as a joke, and I said, "Well, I have to say that a salary of $250,000 a year does seem a lot for a junior-high-school guidance counselor in Raytown." I think we did get mostly straight answers, though, and they indicated that our classmates thought the world had treated them pretty well. Asked if their standard of living had turned out to be better or worse than they had expected when they were at Southwest, only 8 percent of the men and 11 percent of the women said worse; a majority of them said that they had enough money for just about anything they really needed. Asked the same question about their personal life, only 16 percent of the men and 13 percent of the women said it was worse than they had expected. I suspect the results would have been similar at Sequoia High School. We were, after all, dancing to the same music.

But the NBC film about the two classes at Sequoia dealt with some changes in the society in a way that we were barely able to touch in a survey. At the beginning of the NBC film, there are shots of the 1976 graduation ceremony. As the camera plays on the new Sequoia graduates, the commentator, Tom Snyder, says, "Life has a temporary quality for them. Even their caps and gowns are disposable. They don't believe in the work ethic, government, or God, as students did a generation ago, but neither do they have the prejudice, the hang-ups, or the naïveté of that generation. They're more hip in many ways—to themselves and their surroundings. A generation ago, the world was a lot simpler and more secure—at least that's the way it seemed to the graduates of 1953." In the days when Carolyn and Peter and Denny went to Sequoia, it was dominated by the sort of middle-class white students who were likely to go on to college, but it also had students from working-class families and families that still lived a small-town life, even though they were an easy drive from the San Francisco airport. Hearing the demographics described, I was reminded of Southwest. Compared to Southwest, though, it sounded like a much more substantial institution—huge, highly organized, and brimming with what we used to call in those days school spirit. In boys' gym, a standardized physical fitness test was given each year, and for the rest of the year the boys suited out every day in gym shorts whose color designated how they had done—a system of winners and losers that was at least as brutal as anything thought of at Yale. There were four "blocks" of activities, and each block had an elected leader who was called a commissioner, so that Denny began his political career as Commissioner of Boys' Athletics. When he was the president of the school, his official title was Commissioner of Welfare. Sequoia still looked like a considerable institution when I drove by it, despite its loss of bushes. It takes up a vast square block with a rambling, mission-style campus. Except for its size, it looked more or less the way I had imagined it, including the pink stucco and the palm trees. Carolyn Krogh had saved a lot of things from her time there. Looking through her scrapbooks, we came across Denny's election flyer when he was running for Commissioner of Welfare—the head of the whole place. His motto was "Pointing the Way to a Better Sequoia." He was, of course, a shoo-in. According to Carolyn, the Sequoia High School of 1953, like most high schools, was full of cliques, but Denny managed to maintain rapport with all of them.

In the NBC film, a montage of news clips from the early fifties shows the Nixon Checkers speech, and a smiling Dwight and Mamie Eisenhower, and one of Elizabeth Taylor's early weddings, and the wedding of Eddie Fisher and Debbie Reynolds, and a few seconds of Marilyn Monroe entertaining the troops in Korea, and the retirement speech of Joe DiMaggio, the man who taught every male high-school student in the fifties that the whole point was making it look easy. A lot of the pictures in the montage didn't actually reflect a terribly simple and secure world. A mushroom cloud rose above the test explosion of an atomic bomb. Wernher von Braun, the man who had helped design the rockets that terrorized London, spoke in his ominous accent about the development of satellites. Joseph Stalin stood on a reviewing platform—bundled in his greatcoat, waving his oddly awkward little wave. Joe McCarthy glowered as that shrewd pixie Joseph Welch put him away in a few dozen dazzling words about cruelty and forgiveness. But the commentary said, "Things seemed less ambiguous then. There were the good guys and the bad guys. Issues were black and white. It wasn't until later that they became multicolored and mixed with shades of gray."

I think that's true, all in all, although for high-school seniors at places like Sequoia and Southwest in 1953, part of what kept the issues simple was that we didn't spend a lot of time examining them. When the Supreme Court handed down the *Brown v. Board of Education* decision, in the spring of our first year at Yale, I remember being surprised to see Missouri listed among the states whose schools would be affected. I had gone through twelve years of legally segregated education without knowing it. We graduated from high school ten years before there was general recognition among white Americans that discrimination against black people was a problem outside the states of the Old Confederacy—whose own customs were thought of by the rest of the country as deplorable but essentially immutable, like bragging among Texans. A track star who had been among the 1 percent of black students in the Sequoia Class of 1953 was one of the class members interviewed at some length on the NBC film, and I suspect that many of his classmates who thought they had gone out of their way to make him feel welcome were surprised to hear him tell the interviewer that he had, in fact, felt isolated and marginalized. In the second semester of our freshman year at Yale, a particularly bright and engaging black member of our class seemed to fall apart before our eyes and then simply disappeared—reducing the black population of the class, according to my count, by 25 percent. We were as puzzled as the Sequoia graduates must have been at the testimony of the track star. "But everyone was so *nice* to him," people said.

"We had no problems," an actor named Bob Wood from Denny's class told the NBC interviewer. "The world had no problems for us. Our lives were guaranteed—the good life of America." Roles were set, and set for life. When I graduated from high school, I don't believe I knew one person whose parents were divorced. Divorce was something we associated with people like Elizabeth Taylor. But by our twenty-fifth reunion, according to the survey Eddie and I took, a quarter of the people in our class had been divorced at one time or another. Some of the women interviewed in Gavin's film said that in the fifties it was assumed that the destiny of any female who graduated from Sequoia High School was to be a wife and a mother. I suspect many of the women in our class still believed that—only 12 percent of them, as opposed to 66 percent of the men, said that the part of their life that had given them the most satisfaction was work—but by the time of our twenty-fifth reunion, it was common for a medical school class to be half women. Before we had been out of high school fifteen years, sons and daughters of respectable middle-class people would be living in communes, producing offspring with names like Sunshine and Gladness. Young men of similarly respectable backgrounds would be fleeing to Canada rather than serve in their country's armed forces. Could any graduating senior in 1953 whose own striving was aimed toward, say, the law think the day would come when he'd be asked what his own son did and he would answer cheerfully that his son was a chef? Could he imagine that there would be a day when he'd be asked if his daughter was married and he would answer, equally cheerfully, that she and her boyfriend had been living together for a few years but hadn't yet decided whether to tie the knot?

What the Sequoia graduates had come to realize, looking back from the perspective of their early forties, was that the uncomplicated society they had been prepared for had changed so much that where they fit into it had turned out to be painted in those complicated shades of gray. That's a common feeling among people my age, I think, whatever they write on surveys asking them about satisfaction—that somehow the rules got changed in the middle of the game. What made it all the more difficult for some of them was that the rules we were handed had been so simple and clear and presumably not subject to argument or even examination. One of the women from Denny's class—Judy Murphy, identified as someone "into the consciousness movement" who, with her husband, ran a combination coffeehouse and art-film theater—put it succinctly. "I think you had the definitions," she said, "but you found that they didn't work."

As it turned out, Marilyn Montgomery, whose presence on Denny's arm had been part of the vision conjured up by Peter Krogh at the memorial service, was among the Sequoia graduates for whom the rules had apparently not changed in the middle of the game. She was, and is, living in the Chicago suburbs, married to a doctor she met a few years after college. By the time I reached her on the telephone, months after Denny's death, some rumors about him had floated back from California, including the rumor that he had died of AIDS. I told her that Denny had taken his own life. I also told her that for some of us at the memorial service she had been frozen in time as the to-die-for Marilyn Montgomery. Except for a few telephone calls in the year or two after graduation, she'd had no contact with Denny after they left Sequoia, so her memory of him had also been frozen in time. What had particularly stuck with her was how naturally and modestly he carried his schoolboy renown ("He was Mr. Everything, who was still a buddy to the ones who weren't"). She still has the Redwood City *Tribune*'s review of the production that she and Denny were rehearsing for when they posed for the yearbook picture Peter Krogh had shown around after the memorial service—a lightly plotted student musical in which Denny played a cluster of broadly comic parts and she played a red-hot mama named Uwanna Russel. "Television can grab a new comedian right off the stage in Denny Hansen, who had 'em howling in four roles," the review said. The notion of Denny as a slapstick comedian would have astounded his colleagues at the School of Advanced International Studies, of course. I was a little surprised to hear about it myself. In the yearbook of the to-die-for Marilyn Montgomery, Denny had written that his burlesque turns on stage were the happiest moments he had spent at Sequoia. When she reread those words after Denny died, it had occurred to her that they might have been more deeply felt than most things people write in high-school yearbooks. He had excelled at so much and so much had been expected of him, she thought, that it might have been a great relief simply to be goofy for a couple of evenings.

That wasn't the tack Denny took in Mike Gavin's film. Gavin had tracked him down in Washington for one of the interviews of graduates that were done individually, in people's homes or offices. Unlike the others who were singled out, Denny made only one short appearance in the film. He already looked quite a bit thinner than he had as a young man, and he didn't smile at all. I suspect that when his picture flashed across the screen—a picture of the only person in the school whose name and face had been known to everyone at Sequoia—a number of his classmates may have had a moment of doubt about who he was. After that moment, he was identified as Roger D. Hansen, once president of the student body, later Yale undergraduate and Oxford Rhodes Scholar, and now Dr. Roger D. Hansen, a world-trade specialist at Johns Hopkins. He was interviewed in his office at SAIS, where he was spending the year as a visiting professor. What he said, recalling those high-school days, was "My modus operandi was to smile and pretend there were no differences of opinion. Somehow, being nice seemed far more appropriate than it does today."

19

IN the middle seventies, the movement to make some changes in the international economic system picked up steam because of the success of OPEC in quadrupling the price of oil within a few months. There were some people in the commodity-exporting countries of the world who believed that forming what amounted to cartels for raw materials was the way that the less-developed countries were going to exert pressure on the industrialized countries to adopt more favorable trade policies and to share some of the power they held in institutions like the International Monetary Fund and the World Bank. There was wide agreement that, at the least, some attempt should be made to smooth the drastic ups and downs in commodity prices that could devastate the economy of a Third World country. Many of those lobbying for what was sometimes called a new international economic order also believed that foreign aid that worked from the top down—a project, say, that helped build a huge dam in a Third World country on the theory that the building of the dam would involve jobs and the operation of the dam itself would provide the electricity for more industry and therefore more jobs—should be de-emphasized in favor of foreign aid that focused on what was being called "basic human needs."

Among Americans involved in these matters—the North-South Agenda—the rationale offered for change varied widely. Some people maintained that it made economic sense for the North to establish more equitable long-term trade policies with the countries that were presumably going to be customers for the North's manufactured goods. (When I first heard that argument, it struck me as a moral position outfitted in economic clothing for the benefit of the harder noses, but a year or so after Denny died, the lead item in *The New York Times* began, "The American economy, badly in need of bright spots, is gaining strength from an unlikely source: the third world, where purchases of American goods rose 15 percent last year.") Some people said—or believed, even if they didn't quite say it—that the North basically owed the South for having exploited its economies in the past, and that the changes ought to reflect a sort of international economic affirmative action. There were people offering any number of practical arguments for concentrating foreign aid on basic human needs, and there were also people who argued something close to the proposition that basic human needs fell under the rubric of human rights.

All of this seemed at its most intense about the time that Jimmy Carter was elected President, and there was an assumption that the Carter State Department, with its emphasis on human rights, would show some serious interest in the issue. There seemed to be an obvious match between the Carter Administration and Roger D. Hansen, whose papers for the Overseas Development Council had laid out what Ed Morse called an "exquisite overview of the problem." So Denny—who had spent much of the previous dozen years as a sort of itinerant foreign affairs specialist—finally went into government as a senior staff member of the National Security Council.

A classmate of ours named Peter Grose was in the government at the same time, working in State Department policy planning. Shortly after Denny's death, I saw Peter at a class dinner in New York. (The program for the dinner had a nice fifties balance of presentations from members of the class. Peter, who is the executive editor of *Foreign Affairs*, talked about the end of the Cold War. Another classmate showed a movie of the Snowball Riot of 1954, which wasn't a riot by today's standards but was, I might as well acknowledge, what many people in the class have always regarded as the high point of our freshman year. I don't suppose any of us as undergraduates had considered the possibility that the Cold War would ever end, except maybe by means of an exceptionally large explosion that we didn't spend a whole lot of time worrying about. I don't suppose any of us had ever expected the snowball riot to come across as an event reflecting a time that was almost quaintly innocent and outdated; we might almost have been watching films of German students acquiring dueling scars.) As the Carter Administration began, Peter was, by chance, a State Department representative on a committee assigned to prepare a presidential review memorandum—known in the trade as a PRM, which is pronounced "prim"—on Third World economic development. The NSC staffer who was to chair the committee had been described to Peter as a bright young economist from SAIS named Roger D. Hansen. "I hadn't seen Denny since the boat on the way to England," Peter told me. "I might have caught a glimpse of him on the street at Oxford, but we were in different colleges. I remembered him as a great hero—big smile, gregarious, glamorous. I arranged to go to a meeting before the project to see if it was the same guy. He was a bit thinner, but otherwise unchanged—the same gorgeous smile, the same charming, laughing Denny."

It turns out that there are a number of agencies and departments of government that have an interest in Third World economic development—the Pentagon, for instance, and the Treasury Department, and the Agency for International Development—and they all sent representatives to the panel. "In a way, the point of these projects is not the resulting document but the argument that leads up to it," Peter told me. "That's where policy gets shaped." Except that the PRM on Third World development never really got anywhere. As Peter remembers, it eventually got folded into some other PRM. Part of the problem, he thinks, is that Denny seemed to have no idea how to handle such a project. He seemed alternately rigid in his ideas or off in the clouds. Looking back at that time, Denny's friends tend to say that he couldn't translate his ideas into action. "He was not a bureaucratic entrepreneur," Ed Morse told me. "He could address himself brilliantly to ways in which the stability of underdeveloped countries was in the interest of the United States. What he couldn't do was say, 'Here's how to organize the tin market,' or, more seriously, put together the coalition that would push that. The NSC has tremendous power to call meetings, co-opt issues. He was *not* facile at that sort of thing. He was willing to be confrontational. But he didn't like to pick up the phone to do the trading and favor collecting and that sort of thing."

In trying to explain Denny's ineffectiveness as a bureaucrat, two or three of the people I spoke to used the same person as a comparison. I'll call him Joe Smith. Someone with an academic background similar to Denny's, Smith had thrived in at least two Administrations and had then gone off to get rich in the private sector. They told stories about Smith's ability to manipulate, his willingness to bend in one direction or another, his skill and daring at "reaching across the table" to bring things under his control.

Finally, I said, "But he sounds truly dreadful." I felt the need to come to Denny's defense. What was so great about being manipulative? Was I meant to admire someone who was willing to trim his beliefs to fit the next Administration? It sounded as if part of what Denny was being accused of was being uncompromising about what he believed in. Intertwined with my need to defend Denny, I suppose, was the realization that I would have probably been pretty hesitant to reach across the table myself, if some cruel chance had bounced me in the direction of the government.

The person I was talking to thought about my assessment of Smith for a moment. "Yeah, he's fairly awful," he finally said. But Smith was being used for comparison because he was the other extreme, my informant pointed out. There was a position in between—people who were true to their beliefs but had the savvy to make them part of an Administration's policies. "He never really understood how to make policy in the world, to insert himself in the bureaucracy in a manner that could permit him to advance policy along the lines that he wanted it to be advanced," I was told by Robert Pastor, who was in charge of Latin America for the NSC at the time. "He never found out where the levers of power were." Denny apparently showed no indication of understanding that the government's adopting the policy of, say, basing American aid on the priority of basic human needs didn't mean anything unless he had the power to block any aid programs he hadn't signed off on. According to what Ted Geiger had said that night at Tersh's, Denny did understand how the game was played—and how much he was losing by remaining detached from it—but simply couldn't bring himself to jump into the fray.

Also, what was going on in the world was beginning to shove the problems of the less-developed countries off the American foreign policy agenda. "Relations with the Soviets got bad," I was told by Joseph Nye, a Harvard professor (and Rhodes Scholar) who has worked in both academia and government on issues that were close to the ones that engaged Denny. "There was more of a shift toward East-West from North-South. The North-South issue was started really by the oil embargo, and by 1977 the agenda began to change. Détente was breaking down. The Soviets were less cooperative. The Committee for the Present Danger was saying that the United States was Number Two. There was less sympathy for the LDCs. Basically, the subject changed. Also, in the beginning of North-South, there was an exaggeration of the power commodities gave. Now people began to say, 'If there's a cartel in bananas, so what?' There was also a trend away from commodities. People were manufacturing smarter products, and commodities played a smaller role." In a few years, of course, the North-South Agenda was no longer much talked about. The Secretary of State was Alexander Haig, who, as I was reminded by one of the people who had worked with Denny, made his position on the legitimacy of Third World concerns clear by referring routinely to the "so-called Third World."

During the "Big Chill" session at Tersh's, I had been taken aback when one of the State Department people said that Denny's big mistake had been getting involved in the issues of North and South. There we were, after all, discussing someone who had committed suicide—someone with all sorts of serious problems, physical and psychological and maybe even spiritual. It seemed remarkable to me that anyone could think that his problem was having chosen the wrong subsection of international relations. After talking to a lot of people in Denny's field, though, I didn't have any doubt that, even in the heyday of the North-South Agenda, there were people who thought it was a dead end. The approach to international affairs that has dominated the American foreign affairs community for some years is called realism. The realist view of the pressure for a new international economic order in the seventies was summarized to me this way: There has always been inequality among nations, and if we ignore this flapdoodle long enough—meanwhile peeling away some of the more economically successful of these countries, like South Korea—the subject will simply fade away. Among foreign policy academics in America, there were people who began building serious careers in the seventies on the relationship between the industrialized and non-industrialized nations

—particularly on the aspect of the growing interdependence of all countries in such matters as environmental protection and nuclear proliferation—but there were also people who always considered the entire subject essentially secondary and, worse, essentially wet. Even at the height of the interest in North-South, a colleague of Denny's told me, there was some feeling among people who thought of themselves as his mentors that he should stop wasting his time with such issues—that the North-South dialogue was the sort of subject that interested "ex-hippies and women who are worried about babies with diarrhea."

In discussing Denny with people who deal with foreign policy for a living, I got the impression that taking an emotional position based on notions of right and wrong is one of the most embarrassing things that can happen to someone in the field—it seems to be a field whose tone remains planted in the fifties—and people sympathetic to Denny were quick to come to his defense on that score. Although Denny, in Ted Geiger's words, "loved the LDCs," he was otherwise "quite a realist." Geiger says that Denny's book on the North-South Agenda could be described as "a bleeding-heart book not written in bleeding-heart style. If you accept the basic premise, that rich Northern nations have a deep obligation to poor Southern nations, it's a brilliant piece of analysis." Robert Keohane, a Harvard political scientist whose interests overlapped Denny's, reminded me that Denny's premier journal article on the North-South Agenda—a piece called "The Political Economy of North-South Relations," which appeared in *International Organizations* in the autumn of 1975—pointed out that the interests of the more powerful countries of OPEC did not coincide with the interests of the poorer countries, and that the South's efforts to better its position in the trade and economic and monetary machinery of the world would eventually fall apart. "He was sympathetic but he was a good political scientist," Keohane told me. "And political scientists are glinty-eyed at best. They don't confuse their preferences with their expectations."

I don't know what sort of expectations Denny had for getting his preferences across in the Carter Administration, but I suspect that they weren't high. He was ready to leave long before Alexander Haig came into view. He had never really settled in. "His office was never finished," I was told by Riordan Roett, who used to visit Denny fairly often in those days. "It looked kind of like a rented office. There was no art on the walls or anything. It was in the Executive Office Building. I'd go over for lunch at the Navy Mess. Then we'd go back to his office. I'd listen and he'd bitch." Ted Geiger had the same sort of lunches with Denny, except that they took place at a club rather than at the Navy Mess. Geiger urged him to seek an academic post. Looking realistically at the prospects of someone who had difficulty with authority and was often angry and couldn't bring himself to put together coalitions within a bureaucracy, Geiger offered some simple advice: "Get yourself tenured." With the help of Isaiah Frank and Robert Tucker, two of his old teachers, Denny found a spot as the Blaustein Professor of International Organization at SAIS. His career as a senior staff member of the National Security Council had lasted seven months.

Carol Austin believes that Denny's only interest in being

on the National Security Council staff was to prove that he could be appointed—canceling out his rejection by the Foreign Service years before, because of his back or his analysis or whatever, at a time when people like Rocky Suddarth and Warren Zimmerman were going abroad to take up their first posts—and that he wouldn't have had any illusions about what he might accomplish. There are colleagues, though, who talk about Denny's stint in the Executive Office Building the way some of his college friends talk about his years at Oxford—as an experience that must have dealt a severe blow to his self-confidence.

"It's as if a medical doctor who was teaching medical students a specific kind of surgery and then finally had the opportunity to be that kind of surgeon found that he couldn't do it," Bob Pastor has said. "His strength in academia was talking about policy, and then he had a chance to make policy and he just couldn't, and that must have been frustrating." Robert Keohane agrees that when Denny came out of the government "he was very critical of a lot of things going on in the field, but very, very diffident about his own work and insights."

"Did he still smile?" I asked Keohane.

"His smile was always wry," Keohane said. "The smile I remember is a smile that is made with a sardonic reference to somebody who's been very successful in government and Roger thinks is not very deep or in some way is a phony."

Keohane believes that a lack of confidence was partly responsible for Denny's increasing difficulty in writing after *Beyond the North-South Stalemate*, the book he did for the 1980s Project, was completed in 1977. I suppose that there are endeavors in which self-confidence is even more important than it is in writing—tightrope walking comes immediately to mind—but it's difficult for me to think of anybody producing much writing if his confidence is completely shot. In order to take a crack at the third or fourth draft, you have to hold on to an almost insane belief— insane in that you can't think of any rational evidence to support it—that what you're working on, by now stupefyingly boring to you, will be of interest or value to others. "Roger was very perceptive," Robert Keohane told me. "The range of his judgment was very wide. He saw things from many angles. And if someone does that and doesn't have this kind of commitment, this belief in the value of what he's doing—this kind of underlying self-confidence that whatever he's doing must be right because his parents taught him when he was two that it was—then it's difficult. And he was clearly having that kind of writing crisis." *Beyond the North-South Stalemate* was the last book Denny published. His most influential journal articles were written in the seventies. What I hadn't realized in the days following the memorial service was that when he joined the SAIS faculty, at the age of forty-one, his most productive years of publishing scholarship were behind him.

From the outside, Denny still seemed to be functioning pretty well in the early eighties. He had a chair at SAIS. He worked hard. People who were close to him speak of the endless notes he would take on small yellow pads and of the perfectionism with which he approached research and of his insistence on pushing himself, even when he was in pain from his bad back. But he wasn't publishing consistently. He was often in pain. He was obviously troubled about how to deal with his sexual orientation. He had already begun to distance himself from his college friends and the friends from his early days in Washington. This was around the time when he got a letter from the Yale Class of 1957, announcing the twenty-fifth reunion and inviting him to send in the enclosed form to let the rest of us know how his life was going.

20

THE usual book was prepared for our twenty-fifth reunion, and there was the usual range of response. Some people sent a sort of curriculum vitae. Some people sent that and a picture. Some people sent that and a picture and an essay on how they were faring or what they thought of life. Denny was listed with only an address. A lot of the people who offered reflections talked about how much a Yale education had meant to them in later life. A. Whitney Griswold would have been pleased to see that his message about the value of a non-vocational liberal education had, however difficult to sell to editors at the time, remained with people who had been students at Yale when he was president. I was actually among those who could have traced a vocational line from Yale, starting with a summer job at *Time* that had come as a sort of side benefit from the *Yale Daily News*—even if the line happened to go back to the extracurricular part of Yale that Griswold had warned us off of from the start. I suppose my father—who, unlike A. Whitney Griswold, had no revisionist feelings about Stover—could have taken that as an indication that he was right about the value of starting off on an even footing with the sons of industrialists.

What impressed André Schiffrin about the biographical reports that were printed in the twenty-fifth reunion book, he told me some time later, was that so many of our classmates seemed to have become their fathers—if not literally taking over the family business or entering the family law firm, which some of them did, at least stepping into our generation's version of what their fathers had been. You could see André himself that way. He, too, had gone into publishing: for many years, he was the editor in chief of Pantheon, which, by coincidence, had evolved from an exile publishing house co-founded by his father, and he was later the founding editor of the New Press. The other people on the platform on Class Day had done what they might have been expected to do. Richard Arnold, who had delivered as the Ivy Ode a Latin poem he described as an "upstart adulteration of the unsullied Horatian form," had become a judge on the Eighth Circuit Court of Appeals, where he is now chief judge and where, I assume, he has the opportunity to dress up his opinions with a burst of Latin now and then. The class poet, Michael Cooke, became an English professor at Yale and the master of Trumbull College and a poet and a scholar whose interests ranged from Byron to modern Caribbean novelists. He was killed in a car crash on his way home from the office one day in 1990. And me? Had I become my father? He raised me not to become him, of course, but it had often occurred to me that a reporter could do worse than aspire to a standard of behavior reflected in my father's approach to being a grocer—give good weight, refuse to buckle under to pressure from the chain stores, treat with contempt the wartime temptation to get rich by cutting a few corners.

There was also a survey done for the Yale reunion—it was done in conjunction with the Harvard and Princeton reunion classes—and on the question of how our lives had measured up to our expectations it was remarkably similar to the results Eddie Williams and I had gotten at Southwest. Asked to consider everything about their lives, 18 percent of our classmates said they felt "extremely self-fulfilled and satisfied," 64 percent said they felt pretty good, although things could be better, and 13 percent felt unhappy and frustrated. The statistics were pretty much the same for Harvard and Princeton. There was a fourth possible answer to the question of how we viewed our lives; it said simply "a wreck." Nobody from any school checked off that one—although it stands to reason that anyone who did consider himself a wreck might simply keep the survey around for a few days to torment himself with and then throw it away.

The fact that the unhappy and frustrated part of the class formed a tiny minority—a minority, I suspect, that would have included Denny, whether he appeared to us to be doing quite well or not—might be used, I suppose, to refute the picture, popular in literature, of jovial and superficially successful Ivy League graduates convening at a reunion only to expose private frustration and regret and despair. That was not the approach to the survey taken by Larry Kramer, the person in our class asked by the editors of the twenty-fifth reunion book to comment on the responses in a serious way. Larry has written plays and novels and screenplays, but he is probably best known as an ac-

tivist in the public struggle over how to combat AIDS—a
founder of Gay Men's Health Crisis and of ACT-UP, a
group that has taken the arguments to the streets. His essay
began, "When I was at Yale, I was terrified I was a weenie."
He pointed out that, despite the fact that the survey seemed
to reflect a great preponderance of happy and fulfilled people who loved their wives and thought their children were
nearly perfect, more than half the members of the class
hadn't responded to the survey, and nearly half the class
hadn't sent in any biographical information for the individual listings. ("Did they feel they might be weenies too?")
Going through the biographical information that had been
sent in, he quoted passages that indicated a lot more pain
and self-doubt than the numbers on the survey seemed to
indicate. He closed by saying, "The word 'weenie' isn't
used anymore. It's extinct. A good thing, too. Because there
aren't any. There never were."

There are other words used, though—nerd or dweeb or
dork. If the concept of weenieness was truly gone in those
idealistic days of 1970, it has crept back by now. Still, the
Yale that my daughters have attended in recent years is a
vastly more tolerant place than it was when we were there,
and I think the structure that produced winners and
losers—the structure that Bob Mason mentioned that night
at Tersh's as having caused so much suffering among people who grew up in the fifties—has been largely dismantled.
The senior societies still exist, but not at the top of a hi-
erarchy; they seem to exist more or less for people who
are interested in that sort of thing. Despite the difficulties
public education has suffered in recent years, the ratio between high-school and prep-school graduates in a freshman

class is roughly the reverse of what it was when Denny and I arrived. Yale College has a level of ethnic diversity that undergraduates in the fifties could have never imagined. The word "shoe" is unknown as an adjective. Whether these changes—in the society as well as at Yale—have had a deep effect on the people in our class is a different matter. Are we fairly represented by the person who told me in 1970 that if the undergraduates had no word for weenie they were all weenies? Some of us have changed, of course, but speaking as someone who takes it for granted that some of the people whose company he most enjoys must have been weenies in college, I know that those distinctions we made as adolescents will never quite leave us.

The story I treasure about the tenacity of such labels concerns Larry Kramer and another classmate named Henry Geldzahler, who, probably at around the time of that reunion, happened to run into each other at Bigelow's, a Greenwich Village drugstore that used to have a soda fountain where a lot of people in the neighborhood lingered over breakfast. Henry, a close friend of mine all through Yale, was not at first glance cast in the Stover mold. When he was a senior, I described him as looking like Charles Laughton at sixteen. His disdain for competitive sports was branded into my memory by his account of going to summer camp at the age of twelve: "They went to play baseball, I sat in the tent and read a book; they went for a hike in the woods, I sat in the tent and read a book . . ." At Yale, though, he was a popular figure among soccer players as well as members of the Elizabethan Club. After Yale, he became a curator of American art at the Metropolitan

Museum and a sort of uncle to the pop art movement and the Commissioner of Culture of New York and someone whose face constantly shows up in the paintings of David Hockney and others.

"If they could see us now—the people who thought we were weenies at Yale," Larry said to Henry that morning at Bigelow's.

Henry straightened up and said—quite accurately, as it happens—"Nobody thought *I* was a weenie at Yale!"

I was asked to comment on the survey in a manner less serious than Larry's, my role in the class not having altered appreciably in those twenty-five years. I said that my own survey, taken with my usual controls, indicated that after twenty-five years income was precisely in inverse proportion to academic standing in the class—which could be interpreted to mean, although I didn't mention this possibility, that in the long run being smarter than they were didn't do us a lot of good. I talked about a theory that I had actually heard while asking people at Yale in 1970 to explain a fact that had fascinated me: The most outraged and venomous response to the turmoil of the late sixties was not from entrenched Old Blues who had graduated in the twenties or thirties but from young men who graduated in classes within a year or two of our own. There were a number of theories used to explain this—theories having to do with the non-political mentality of the Eisenhower years and the fact that the mid-fifties graduates were still struggling for the positions in life that the students had dismissed as worthless—but the theory I liked best held that alumni from the mid-fifties classes suspected that the world of rebellious students included lewd and excessive sexual activity, and the thought of having missed such goings-on by only a few years was driving them to distraction. I also said that the sort of question I had wanted to see on the survey was "Do your thoughts tend to dwell morbidly on the future of your prostate?" When I reread what I had written in the twenty-fifth reunion book, it did occur to me that if my father had been able to read it in Denny's presence, he might have said once again, "If I thought he believed any of that, I'd have him shot."

21

SOMEBODY I talked to in Washington said that among respectable academic institutions the Nitze School of Advanced International Studies of Johns Hopkins must be about as far from Magdalen College, Oxford, as you can get. Nobody has ever talked of it as a quiet refuge, away from the hustle and bustle, where scholars can concentrate on the pure search for truth. It is consciously in the hustle and bustle. In fact, many of its professors apparently would like nothing better than to be further in. Unlike, say, professors of English who specialize in John Milton—none of whom have hopes of actually *becoming* John Milton the next time an Administration changes—a number of them are interested in being practitioners of foreign policy as well as scholars. SAIS was founded in 1943 by practitioners such as Christian Herter and Paul Nitze, and it affiliated with Johns Hopkins, whose principal campus is sixty miles away, only after seven years of independent operation. An overwhelming majority of its students are interested in applied rather than academic international relations; they need a master's degree for a job, in government or maybe in an international bank. Many of them are attracted to SAIS partly because it is well situated for arranging internships in Washington that may lead to valuable experience and valuable contacts. The offices and classrooms are in the building where Denny's memorial service was held—an early-sixties box that looks as if it might be the headquarters of some industry's Washington lobby—or in a building down the street that had previously been, in fact, the home of the National Forest Products Association. The campus was described by one student I spoke to as "a pool table and two vending machines." A number of students are at SAIS for only a year, since they spend the other year at the SAIS campus in Bologna. A number of them are foreigners. Many of them hold jobs while they go to school. All in all, the atmosphere is, in the words of one student, "crushingly transient."

SAIS is not the sort of place where someone whose specialty is international economics might have lunch at the faculty club with a colleague from the English department. The English department is in Baltimore, along with the rest of Johns Hopkins. There isn't any faculty club. Faculty members, like the students, are scattered around Washington. Among similar schools—the Fletcher School at Tufts, Woodrow Wilson at Princeton, the Georgetown School of Foreign Service—SAIS has a reputation for faculty bickering, although, someone assured me, "it is not polarized, it is atomized—a collection of individual entrepreneurs." The fund-raising at SAIS seems to emphasize endowed chairs, and maybe because of that there seems to be a heightened consciousness of a professor's public role. A large section of the bulletin board in the lobby is devoted to press mentions of faculty and graduates—an alumnus quoted in a *Christian Science Monitor* think piece on the Middle East, say, or a professor's by-line on an op-ed piece in *The Washington Post*. I got the impression that it's the sort of place where an appearance on the *MacNeil/Lehrer NewsHour* is highly valued, and an appearance on *Nightline* is valued even more.

"In a place like that, the imperative is that you contribute," Riordan Roett has said of SAIS. Even as late as the middle eighties, it was possible to read a curriculum vitae of Roger D. Hansen and see him as a busy and productive member of the foreign affairs community—a member of the board of editors of *International Organizations*, the chairman of the international relations department at SAIS—but apparently a number of Denny's colleagues saw him as someone who was not contributing. He did not present papers regularly at academic conferences; he was not seen on the op-ed pages. He had worked hard on the book about American foreign policy—its premise was that the détente of the Nixon years was not true détente but a sort of charade—and apparently the Hopkins press had expressed some interest in publishing it if he added some chapters and made some changes. But he wasn't willing to do the revisions. Sooner or later, he began to lose interest in the book. Maybe he thought that the moment for discussing Nixonian détente had passed. Maybe, applying his usual exacting standards, he had decided that the book was simply not good enough. For one reason or another, Denny in the last years of his life made no serious effort to get his principal work of the decade published. "For an academic this is ruinous for one's self-confidence," George

Liska said after Denny's death. "Not being able to put the finishing touches on a book and send it into the world."

In a way, I suppose, Robert Tucker was being rather generous at the memorial service when he said that the expectations that he and George Liska had for Denny after having taught him were not disappointed. Denny's production as a member of the faculty must have been a disappointment. In his first decade at SAIS, his reputation as a teacher was spotty—his classroom performance, one colleague told me, made more difficult by his stutter.

"Stutter!" I said. "Denny didn't stutter."

Apparently Roger did. Other members of the faculty confirmed it. Riordan Roett said that as far as he could recall the stutter began in the late seventies and was off-and-on, depending on the circumstances and Denny's frame of mind. His frame of mind was often not good at faculty meetings. Politically, he was a bit to the left of most of the faculty—his view on Vietnam, as remembered by Carol Austin, was that "we ought to run for the shore and then, when we got on the boats, we ought to give them the finger"—but policy differences were not the cause of Denny's estrangement from most of his colleagues. (Apparently, feuds at SAIS rarely have to do with policy differences.) "He had rigid views of what was moral and what was immoral, what was principled and what was not principled," George Liska has said. "But the criteria were not always easily inferable. It was not always easy to know which way he'd jump." He was thought of as overly punctilious, and suffering from a scrupulosity so strong that anyone who was a point or two off the absolutely straight and narrow could be dismissed as a hopelessly corrupt human being.

As we had suspected at the memorial service, the SAIS people, by and large, had been completely unaware of the existence of the Denny Hansen that Peter Krogh and Pudge Henkel had talked about ("None of us knew those glorious beginnings he had," Liska says). The person known to the faculty was intense and judgmental and certainly not known for his smile. When he took a medical leave after his second back operation, in the late eighties, it was assumed by some on the faculty that "he was hoping to get away from us" and would not be back—a possibility that a number of his colleagues would have apparently welcomed. I assume that by then Denny would have been happy to be elsewhere. On the other hand, there was obviously a shortage of prominent academic institutions in the market for a professor in his fifties whose last book had been published in 1979. Denny had a chair at SAIS. He had a reasonable teaching load. Denny and the School of Advanced International Studies appear to have been locked in a mutually irritating embrace.

"I guess toward the end of his life he could be a real pain in the neck," I said to Ed Morse one day in New York. Morse now runs the *Petroleum Intelligence Weekly*, a newsletter for the oil business. He seems to retain a lot of affection for Denny, even though their last contact amounted to Morse's showing up for a dinner date at a Georgetown apartment Denny was then living in only to be told by the doorman that Denny had left for New York. Morse said that Denny had indeed made no secret of his belief that SAIS was a corrupt academic environment. "He thought the people who ran it were cynical," Morse said. "And he thought that the professors were interested in their little fiefdoms rather than teaching, not interested in collegial relationships, not interested in spending time with students, toward whom they had an incredibly patronizing and condescending attitude." With these views, Denny probably did seem rigid and arrogant and moralistic, Morse said, but "on the other hand, he was right."

I honestly hadn't thought of that: he was probably right. However moralistic his views or choleric his behavior, he had made what another professor with long experience at SAIS later described to me as a "sound assessment of the institution." In any organization, the person who is always drawing moral distinctions and condemning people for having strayed from absolute rectitude is a pain in the neck, and what makes him so is often that he's at least partly right. I'm sure you could make a case that some of Denny's colleagues were scholars of scrupulous intellectual honesty and serious commitment to their students. All in all, though, I figured that he was probably right—I figured that his difficulties with his colleagues were, as Tucker had said at the memorial service, mainly the result of "his fierce defense of principles of right conduct as he saw them"— and I was proud of him for it. For that matter, I was proud of him for loving the LDCs, at the risk of being taken for a bleeding heart who worried about babies with diarrhea.

By the time I talked to Morse, I had heard a lot of people tell me what a drag Denny had become in his last years. People had told me of his erratic moralism at SAIS. People talked of having run into him on the street or in the supermarket and, with one casual question about how he was, having set off a litany of complaints, physical and psychological. (Carol Austin's view of why Denny had transformed himself into a thin person was that the robust California swimmer's body of the Denny we had once known was simply a bad body to kvetch in: "If you have the soul of a poet and really feel miserable, the worst thing is to look great—healthy, vital, robust. Where's your credibility? He used to tell me about the passage in *La Bohème* that deeply moved him. Mimi is on the sofa, dying, and her muff falls and rolls along the stage. He thought of himself as Mimi.") I suppose I had been feeling sad that —completely aside from the question of happiness, completely aside from the question of worldly success—Denny may have in the last years of his life got to the point at which people winced when they saw him approaching.

I preferred the picture of Denny as the incorruptible— and, yes, irritating—moralist who happened to be right. This was, after all, Denny Hansen we were talking about. I know he was difficult in his personal relationships. "One of the things in life you have to do is to negotiate interpersonal relationships," Carol Austin had said to me. "He hadn't learned to negotiate in the family, and he never really learned. He was not a compromising personality: he couldn't seem to learn that people may be good people even though you disagree with them on this or that." But I preferred to accept the explanation she offered for that: "He was picky about people, but he had strong standards and ideals. He had good taste in people." She had said one other thing that I tried to keep in mind as I heard complaints about Denny's behavior—some of them from her.

She said, "I think he was genuinely worthwhile." I once wrote an obituary of a colleague—he was a hard case for whom I had a lot of respect and affection—and it ended with a quote from the person who had been closest to him at his death: "He made it difficult, but he was worth the trouble." I preferred to think that of Denny.

22

BY the early eighties Denny had cut himself off from his Yale friends and the friends he had made during those early years in Washington—or maybe that was when his friends became aware of what had happened. It was a period when things seemed to get worse and worse for Denny. His temper got worse. His physical condition got worse. He had two serious back operations and a serious shoulder injury, and he remained in pain that seemed to get worse rather than better. His perfectionism got worse. The shoulder injury was the result of a weight-lifting accident when, according to someone who was in the gym at the time, he tried to bench-press so much weight that his arm simply snapped. I had assumed that the exercise he did was partly physical therapy for his injured back, but in fact it was despite his injured back. The running, particularly, exacerbated his problem. The list of colleagues he considered morally fit for normal conversation got smaller and smaller. His scrupulosity was also directed toward himself, of course, and in the words of someone who knew him well, "He found himself a little wanting."

Although I'm certain the matter wouldn't have come up in any dinners he had chosen to have with old friends, he was apparently finding coming to grips with his sexual identity a great agony. Emerging from college in 1957 may have been good timing in any number of ways, but for those among us who were gay, it seems to me, the timing could hardly have been worse. Talk about the rules changing in the middle of the game! A gay male born twenty years before us probably, unless he happened to be in certain lines of work, remained in the closet his entire life—playing his role in a marriage of convenience or regarded as a "confirmed bachelor." A gay male who was born twenty years after Denny would probably just be gay—if he lived in a large city, at least. Men of our age grew up in a period in which someone who felt a homosexual attraction was likely to believe himself afflicted by a heinous maladjustment whose cure was unknowable—particularly unknowable to someone who couldn't bear to mention the condition to another human being. Around the time of our fifteenth reunion, the reunion at which everyone is presumed to have slipped into the slot he will occupy from then on, society's views on the subject had supposedly changed—although that must have been difficult to believe for someone who had grown up not simply hearing his closest friends tell faggot jokes but maybe even telling a few faggot jokes himself.

A few months after Denny's death, my younger daughter started collecting information on the fifties view of homosexuality; she was writing a paper on the subject for a class at Yale. She had grown up in the era that students of gay liberation would refer to as post-Stonewall—a reference to a gay bar in Greenwich Village where patrons responded to a police raid, in the summer of 1969, by fighting back and creating what became a sort of gay Bastille. Our daughters were brought up a few blocks from the Stonewall, in a neighborhood that has had a laissez-faire attitude toward sexual and political and racial variations since early in the century. They have never known a time when their family's friends did not include openly gay people. Trying to answer her questions about the views we held in the fifties made me feel a bit like someone from Salem, thirty years after the unfortunate trials there, trying to explain how, in the context of the times, an outbreak of witchcraft did seem to be a rather logical explanation of what was going on in town.

I believe that when I arrived in New Haven, in the fall of 1953, I would have taken it for granted that I had never run across an actual live homosexual, any more than I had ever run across anybody who took drugs. In high school, we sometimes called people fairies or queers or homos—the word "faggot" was unknown to me before I arrived in the East—but we called them that in the spirit that a sheriff I once met while reporting a story in Missouri, maybe a hundred and twenty miles from where I grew up, said to a student demonstrator who remained limp on the floor after he had been ordered to move off to jail, "Well, just lay there, you damn Comm-a-nuss." The sheriff was not accusing the student of following the line put forth by Marx and Engels and Lenin; he could have as easily called the student a yellow dog. When we called somebody a fairy, the implication was not that he actually engaged in homosexual acts. We just wanted to say something mean. We didn't know any more about the details of a homosexual act than the sheriff knew about the economic theories of Karl Marx.

When I was at Yale, I told my daughter, it wouldn't have been accurate to say that we were homophobic—a word that was not needed in the language at that time, since nearly everybody, at least publicly, was assumed to be homophobic. The subject was simply not in our frame of reference. If I had been asked in, say, 1956 if there was such a thing as homosexuality, I think I would have said, "Of course. I've read about it." We were all familiar with the findings of the Kinsey report—a report that had been published in 1948 and must have provided some mild titillation during our high-school years—that something like 10 percent of American males were homosexuals. But if I had been asked if I knew any homosexuals, I wouldn't have even known enough about such matters to answer, "Not that I'm aware of" or "None who've announced." After I had talked to only a handful of people who were Rhodes Scholars with Denny, I realized that at least three of the Class of 1957 Rhodes Scholars were gay—a fact that should have been predictable, somebody pointed out, since three out of thirty-two amounted to roughly the Kinseyan 10 percent. It has gradually sunk in that Kinsey was not talking about 10 percent of some statistical them. He was talking about 10 percent of us.

If I had been asked in college what homosexuals were like, I would have taken it for granted that these theoretical creatures were effeminate or odd. As the people gathered in Tersh Boasberg's living room that evening had recalled, students at a place like Yale in the fifties couldn't have conceived of the possibility that the breezy, popular varsity swimmer we half expected to become President of the United States might have been gay. After talking to a lot of people who knew Denny in his last years, it seems to me that even after he began moving in gay circles in Washington he had difficulty conceiving of it himself. "I got the feeling that so many of you guys got pickled in aspic concerning what was expected of you," Diana Thomson said, when I visited her and Jim in Cambridge to talk about Denny. "People are so affected by what they were in those college years. Those years are hard to put behind you, no matter how society changed. And I think the more successful you were in college, the harder it is. That's what happened to Denny. He would have been better off if he had been a weenie at Yale. Instead, he was the embodiment of what you were supposed to be."

23

EVEN for someone who wasn't the embodiment of everything we were supposed to be, the realization that you were gay—or, as Denny put it to Ted Geiger, that you were in danger of becoming a homosexual—in a world that, by common consent, had no homosexuals must have been horrifying. By now, of course, a sort of literature of the pre-Stonewall closet is being formed—tales of guilt and shame and disbelief and denial and, for some, the long-shot hope of being "cured." In *Cures*, the historian Martin Duberman, who graduated from Yale College in 1952, writes that while he was an undergraduate he sneaked off to the New Haven Green—which he had heard was a "hangout for fairies"—and then, after some furtive fondling, "ran out of the park, ran without stopping, panicked, hysterical, ran for my life back to my dorm room. I stayed in the shower for hours, cleaning, cleaning. I actually washed my mouth out with soap, though I hadn't used my mouth—other than to make a prayerful pact with God that if he let me off this time, I'd never, *never*, go near the Green again."

The review of *Cures* in *The Nation* was written by Andrew Kopkind. I met Andy when Charlie Trippe, then an officer on the business side of the *Yale Daily News*, arranged to bring the editors of all the Ivy League newspapers to New Haven to discuss the possibility of publishing a magazine called *Ivy*. (As I remember the *Ivy* meeting, Andy, the editor of the Cornell *Sun*, was the one person to bring up the possibility that a magazine for the Ivy League could give the impression of exclusivity and snootiness—an observation that left Charlie, who was presumably counting on precisely that to fuel the advertising revenues, looking puzzled.) Andy and I became close friends, and for a few years after college, we talked about starting a weekly newspaper together in San Francisco—although we never got to the point of figuring out who would look after the business side of it. My wife, Alice, happened to spend a month or so in Los Angeles, where Andy was working, a year before we were married, and she became close friends with Andy instantly. In his review of Martin Duberman's book, Andy talked a bit about his own experience with cures in the days when, as he put it in the review, "the theology of heterosexuality offered the only hope of earthly salvation." Having, as he reported, run afoul of the laws against sexual perversity in Los Angeles in 1964, he was sent by his employer to a psychiatrist to be cured. (This would have been about a decade before the American Psychiatric Association removed homosexuality from its list of mental disorders. An orthodox Freudian of the sort Denny started analysis with at around the same time would have believed homosexuality to be a disorder caused by developmental problems in infancy—meaning that a gay male who was still a gay male after undergoing analysis would presumably have felt worse about himself than he had to begin with.) As it happened, a temporary assignment made airplane commutation the only way for Andy to get to the sessions—and that led to what he called a little therapeutic homework: "My assignment was to sit next to any female passenger I found remotely attractive (or, failing that, approach a stewardess) and try for a pickup. I rehearsed opening lines ('Do you fly the eight o'clock shuttle often?') and the psychiatrist assumed the 'role' of pickupee to my pickupper."

Andy dropped the homework and the psychiatrist and, soon after that, the employer. I didn't know about any of this at the time. Until the early seventies, I knew no more about Andy's sexual orientation than I knew about Denny's. It was several years after that before Andy and Alice and I could discuss the subject openly, and we finally heard the story of his shuttle flights. Andy had gone through his troubles with the law, secretly and alone, during the summer that he and Alice were seeing each other almost daily in Los Angeles; she was horrified when she realized that she had been of no use to someone she cared for. I had a similar response, although when we first heard the story I couldn't help suggesting to Andy that the psychiatrist, perhaps a bit of a klutz with women himself, may have realized that he had a wordsmith of some talent available and hoped to use the opportunity to acquire some deft pickup lines. When Andy came out, what had particularly disturbed me, of course, was that I could have made remarks that hurt him during all of those years when homosexuality did not exist except in the pages of the Kinsey report. I've managed to dredge up a few of those remarks from my memory; so, alas, has he. Alice and Andy and I are still good friends, but the last time he and I discussed all this he acknowledged that he and the man he has lived with for the past twenty years, the filmmaker John Scagliotti, spend most of their time with people they met post-Stonewall—people whose friendship was not embedded in a different era, before the rules changed.

Among people our age, such matters often didn't get discussed openly until ten or fifteen years after Stonewall. (By the late eighties, in *The American Oxonian* class notes, one member of the Class of 1957 noted how many friends he had lost to AIDS, and another referred openly to a companion named Chuck.) For fifties people who turned out to be gay, the years before that must have been a difficult time of transition. It was not clear just how far the rules had changed and who might still be playing by the old rules; it isn't always clear today. Some of our contemporaries came out immediately and many came out selectively—to new friends, say, but not to old friends, or to college friends but not to family—and some came out years later, or not at all. Some spent those transition years trying their best to practice what Andy Kopkind had called the theology of heterosexuality, and some managed to escape the furtive encounters Duberman described and live the personal life that suited them. "What Roger did about it," I was told by one of his friends in Washington who had to face the same transition, "was to batten down for twenty years and see a lot of psychiatrists."

Among people who were familiar with this aspect of Denny's life, a few opinions are universally held. One is that what he wanted more than anything was what he had wanted in those years with Carol Austin and what most people want, whatever era they grow up in—a lasting relationship, a person he could share his life with. Another is that, even after the rules began to change, he had difficulty accepting the possibility that a gay man could integrate his social and professional life. Another is that he was never at ease in the gay community of Washington. A few days after Denny's memorial service, I had a talk about all this with a man I'll call Daniel, who met Denny while exercising at the Y. After having made a remark that assumed Denny was gay, Daniel had received a ferociously angry letter from Denny, upbraiding him for his presumption but, oddly enough, ending with the suggestion that they talk sometime. From what Daniel recalled, that talk and a number of subsequent talks he had with Denny revolved around a problem that had never occurred to me: people our age who had, as Denny's friend put it, battened down for twenty years tended to emerge tentatively into a world they found puzzling. It was a world that people like Daniel, who was twenty years younger and had been openly if quietly gay for all his adult life, took for granted. "It turned out that he needed some help just knowing how to act," Daniel told me. "How to dress. 'Don't wear those pants. Don't worry if you're in a bad mood and you went to the bar and nothing happened.' " In Daniel's view, the advice had limited impact. Denny, he thinks, was never able to operate effectively in what amounted to a subculture with its own customs and rules and hierarchies.

I don't mean that Denny had no friends in the gay community. Daniel remembers many happy evenings of joking and talking about the 49ers over dinner with his companion and Denny. Denny himself lived with somebody off and on for a couple of years. In the mid-eighties Denny became acquainted with one of the gay people in his own field—Scott Thompson, another college golden boy of the fifties, who had been the president of the student body at Stanford and had gone to Oxford as a Rhodes Scholar and had spent some of the transition years married to the daughter of Paul Nitze, a founder of SAIS who has been so generous in his support that his name was eventually added to the official name of the school. Thompson says he tried to interest Denny in participating more in a social scene that might include his intellectual and professional peers, and that Denny, in a tentative way, had acquired a small circle of such friends by the late eighties. Still, the possibility of, say, showing up at a SAIS reception with a male companion or discussing such issues with his colleagues at SAIS was for him unthinkable. There is an argument to be made, I'm sure, that Denny's inability to merge his personal and professional lives—as well as his problems operating in the gay subculture—were indications that he had never, in fact, fully accepted his sexual orientation. ("It was clear to me that Roger couldn't come to grips with it," I was told by an old friend of Denny's to whom Denny had announced that he was gay. "He was so into his era that he hated himself for being gay.") On the other hand, Washington is a conservative place, dominated by an industry that inspires wariness in people who are different in any way, and the wariness has often proved to have been justified.

Like some other gay friends of Denny's I talked to, Daniel had been upset by the obituary in *The Blade*—not because he thought it was inappropriate for an obituary to appear in a gay newspaper, but because the piece had, after a paragraph mentioning Denny's membership in such established organizations as the Council on Foreign Relations and the Cosmos Club, quoted a "friend" as saying, "He also enjoyed dancing at The Eagle and the Chesapeake House." The Chesapeake House, Daniel said, was the sort of place where the only dancing was done by go-go boys and the customers were mainly older men, some of whom might strike a private arrangement with one of the dancers late in the evening; he doubted if Denny had been a regular customer. Denny apparently did show up now and then at The Eagle. Daniel described it as a Levi's-and-leather bar that was, in reality, much tamer than the clothing of its customers would suggest—although it had been named after a fierce avian predator, he told me, some people in the gay community referred to it as the Parakeet Lounge —and was not known as a place to dance. Daniel thought the line about Denny's dancing had made a caricature out of a highly reserved person who didn't happen to be the dancing type.

Some of Denny's gay friends believe that his adult life was, as one of them put it, "largely the story of his struggle with his sexuality." In Andy Kopkind's view, being gay in the fifties—keeping this unspeakable secret, having thoughts that everyone knew were sick and disgusting— could lead to behavior that superficially doesn't have any connection with sexual orientation, like excessive secretiveness about all aspects of life. It could darken problems that were common throughout the population—so that even now gay males are overrepresented in the statistics for teenage suicide and gay males often seek psychiatric help for low self-esteem. When I mentioned some aspects of Denny's behavior to Andy—the telephone early-warning device, for instance, or the hypochondria—I sensed him beginning to nod in recognition before I had finished the sentences. For some of the people gathered in Tersh Boasberg's living room, finding out that Denny had been gay basically offered an explanation of what had happened to his life. They assumed that as he began to face the facts of his sexual orientation—perhaps at Oxford, perhaps through some incident that could not be denied—he realized that he could never cope with the contradiction between the fifties hero he seemed to be and the gay man he knew he was, or, as one of his gay friends put it, he could never fit into the "poisonous template" of the fifties.

There is no way to sort out how much of a role any of this played in the state of mind that eventually led Denny to take his own life, but it's possible that Denny's career was affected by his sexual orientation in at least one specific way. Jim Thomson told me that in the early sixties, when he was working at the State Department, Denny came to him about the problem that was holding up a Foreign Service appointment. He didn't talk about his bad back or about his analysis. He said that the father of another American he had known in Oxford had told the State Department that Denny was a homosexual—an accusation, Denny assured Jim, that was, of course, preposterous. The father was a man of some prominence, but even an accusation from an ordinary citizen would probably have done the trick. In the McCarthy era of our high-school years, I was reminded by seeing John Scagliotti's documentary *Before Stonewall, The New York Times* regularly carried headlines like PERVERTS CALLED GOVERNMENT PERIL and 126 PERVERTS DISCHARGED. Even after John Kennedy took over the White House, the response of Dean Rusk to being advised during a State Department news conference that the building was being picketed by homosexuals was to announce that fact and then, after the laughter died down, to say, "The policy of the department is that we do not employ homosexuals knowingly and that if we discover homosexuals in our department we discharge them." Thomson, who presumably took it for granted that the accusation was in fact preposterous, remembers phoning whomever he knew in personnel to vouch for Denny, and as far as he can recall, that was the last he heard about it.

Not being able to get into the Foreign Service must have been a serious setback for Denny at a time when he seemed to have lost the momentum of his youth, and I suspect that some of the people who accept the trajectory model of Denny's life would say that the motor began to sputter right there—when the accusation to the State Department confirmed his secret fears that the life of limitless possibilities supposedly open to him could never really be. On the other hand, it isn't clear that the accusation was something that actually had been made, as opposed to something Denny feared might be causing his problems with the Foreign Service. In those days, going through a Freudian analysis might have been enough to keep somebody out of the Foreign Service all by itself. Also, was the Foreign Service where Denny truly belonged? Was a man who applied scrupulous moral standards to every decision of every person he came in contact with really cut out to be a diplomat?

24

———

"THE 1980s have not been kind to me," Denny wrote in March of 1990, in a letter thanking a professor at another university for assistance in the search process that had resulted in the hiring of two new faculty members whose duties included replacing the retiring Robert Tucker, Denny's mentor. "Three rounds of back surgery and some reconstruction shoulder work have resulted in a lost decade and a mental state bordering on clinical depression. Also temporarily lost in the process has been the capacity to write—the concentration has just not come back." Because of the prospect of working with the two colleagues, Denny said, "For the first time in several years I can think of SAIS without feeling at least mildly depressed. With Bob's retirement this summer I am losing my only close personal and professional friend on our esteemed faculty."

Looking into Denny's life at SAIS, I couldn't help thinking how far it was from the academic life that had been offered up to Rhodes Scholars at Oxford as a model. What struggles! Within a couple of years in the late eighties, he had a terrible row concerning some curriculum revision and another terrible row concerning the search for someone to teach Soviet studies and a row concerning his own chair that was so serious he was shifted around to another chair. There was some feeling that Denny had alienated the donors of the original chair by straying from the field of international organization toward international relations in the courses he offered, and by not being sufficiently attentive to them. Denny's view was that the entire field of international organization had shifted, and that being more attentive to them would be futile since "they wanted at a minimum Henry Kissinger, and they got me." SAIS struck me as perhaps not the best institution to be in if you happened to be wounded. "They all essentially hate each other," one student told me. "But he was more vulnerable."

It's easy to get a picture of Denny in the later part of the eighties doing nothing much but arguing with his colleagues or stewing by himself in Georgetown. But that wasn't exactly true. Apparently, he became a better teacher in the eighties than he had been. His interests had turned from policy to theory, and his course entitled "Neo-liberalism: International Relations in the 21st Century" was filled to the maximum allowable number of students. I ran across a letter he had written in April of 1990 to the director of a university press, talking about the possibility of doing a book that grows out of "wrestling with a problem that has two levels: (1) Understanding the Kantian/ Comtean elements in international relations at present as an historical event/evolution and (2) understanding why international relations 'theory' (realism, structural realism, neo-liberalism and Keohane's new institutionalism) can tell us so little about the emergence of the 'League of Perpetual Peace' that Michael Doyle and recent events have so dramatically called to our attention." There follows a dense page or so of highly abstruse international-relations theory that doesn't sound at all as if it came from a man who had just lost a decade—although it ends with what I take it had become a sort of characteristic Denny demur, in this case an admission that he might be engaged in "outlining a book which has the misfortune of addressing the general IR reader with a bit too much theoretical discussion, and addressing the IR theorist with not quite enough to convince."

But by the autumn of 1990, one of Denny's acquaintances told me, "life had become incredibly grim to him." Denny seemed to be putting a lot of energy into teaching, but he was no longer involved in the sort of activities that normally engage academics who want to remain in the forefront of their field. He had resigned from the board of the journal *International Organizations*. He had quit going to conferences. He was apparently in terrible pain from his back. He was not convinced that the doctors treating him had done everything that could have been done to alleviate his suffering, and he had spent some time in the latter part of the eighties telling them so. He was taking a lot of medication, and the medication made it impossible for him to concentrate. Despite his back, he continued to swim and run. He and Jim Robinson, his research assistant, would play tennis regularly, but Robinson found it a trial. "There were times when he would start in a terrible mood, and I'd say, 'You're not really enjoying this and neither am I,'" Robinson told me. "And he would switch immediately to the charming Roger. He could do that instantly. That's why most people at SAIS never knew quite how bad things were. They'd come in the office, he'd be fine. They'd leave, and he'd go back to a funk." Charming Roger? Yes. I'm convinced that, even toward the end, there were flashes of Denny in Roger, just as there had been flashes of Roger in Denny.

Toward the end of 1990, Denny was pretty much alone. According to Scott Thompson, who ran into him at a Christmas party, "he said, 'I've been in such a deep hole you couldn't see out of it.' I said, 'Why didn't you call?' But, of course, if you can do that you're not in a depression." He answered the telephone even less than he had in the past. He left the house mainly to go to his psychiatrist's office or to classes he had to teach at SAIS. As Tersh had said that evening, Denny had by then withdrawn from just about everybody he knew. Except for an occasional exchange of letters with his Aunt Norma, he had completely lost touch with his family. His friends from Yale and Oxford and his early days in Washington had faded from his life years before. The young man he had lived with for a while had moved to California. About the only person he saw regularly other than his students was Jim Robinson. A quiet, thoughtful young man, Robinson is somewhat older than most of the students at SAIS; when he came to work on a doctorate in international affairs, he already had a doctorate in European intellectual history. Except for the tennis games and an occasional sandwich at lunch, Robinson's contacts with Denny had to do with research and teaching, but increasingly he was the person Denny phoned when his mood was dark. In early October of 1990, Denny called Robinson and said that the doctors were saying that another back operation would be necessary, one that would result in his being in a body cast for months. "He said that suicide was the logical thing," Robinson told me. In the manner of a professor challenging a graduate student to offer alternate explanations for a theory that was patently correct, Denny said there were no sensible options.

Robinson could think of some options, including a lot of different sorts of treatment that might help alleviate some of the pain, but Denny didn't show any more interest in them than he had in the proposals to revise his book on détente in a way that might make it publishable. For a while, he had a gun, which his psychiatrist apparently persuaded him to get rid of. When Robinson returned to Washington after the Christmas holidays, Denny told him of having taken an overdose of pills on New Year's Day in an effort to kill himself. He had succeeded in blanking out two or three days and, apparently from staggering around the house in a drugged state, in cutting his face and badly burning his hand. After that, Robinson says, Denny talked about a methodical search he had undertaken for a weekend place with a garage that he could rent. He said that he intended to end his life with carbon monoxide.

Around that time, Denny bumped into an old friend, Dora Richardson, while shopping at the Safeway in Georgetown. They had met during the era when Denny was keeping company with Carol Austin ("He was just a charming professor; we got along famously"), and as his health seemed to get worse they had talked from time to time about her belief that psychic pain sometimes gets transferred to physical pain because it's easier to deal with.

In the detergent section of the Georgetown Safeway that day in January, they talked for perhaps an hour. He told her about the suicide attempt and about the possibility of trying again. Then the conversation would shift, and he would ask how she'd been, and inquire about her kids. Denny said he couldn't run and he couldn't work. He said that he had tried all sorts of anti-depressants, with no effect. She told him that he should be hospitalized until the dosage of an anti-depressant could be worked out, and he said the doctor had said the same thing. "I wanted to say, 'You *have to* do it,' " she told me, when we spoke about that day. "But I knew at that point it was like playing games to have said something like that to Roger." A couple of days later, Denny phoned Scott Thompson to see if he could borrow Thompson's weekend house at Rehoboth Beach for a couple of days. He knew it had a garage.

Thompson, who lives in Washington but teaches at the Fletcher School, at Tufts, was in Boston and, of course, knew nothing of Denny's New Year's weekend or his talks about suicide with Jim Robinson and Dora Richardson. He arranged for Denny to pick up the key from a friend. Denny had a class at SAIS that day, and Robinson saw him in his office after it was over. Oddly enough, Robinson says, Denny's classes were still going very well. As he left for home, Denny seemed upset when Robinson couldn't find some papers needed for the following week's class. By the time Robinson reached home there were two messages on his machine—one in a near panic, the second saying that Denny had found the papers among his own things. The next time Robinson heard anything about Denny was the following Tuesday, when Denny's psychiatrist phoned to say that Denny, who had never missed a session before, had not shown up at the appointed time. Robinson went to Denny's house and, in a neat pile on the living-room table, found the instructions for Tersh and the financial papers and a letter for Norma Hansen. After consultation with the psychiatrist, Robinson called the police and reported Denny missing.

Another Washington friend of Scott Thompson's was supposed to use the Rehoboth Beach house the next weekend, but he couldn't find Denny to get the key. Finally, Thompson, from Boston, called a Rehoboth Beach realtor, who found the lights on in the house and a note in the bedroom, and called the police. A police officer broke into the garage. Denny's Honda was parked there, and its ignition was turned on. There was a book and a frying pan on the gas pedal. Denny was lying on the floor of the garage. According to the police report, the officer phoned Scott Thompson, who said, among other things, that the "victim had been 'depressed all of his life.' "

25

WHAT struck me about the will Tersh had drawn was
how close it was to a will that might have been made
by Denny rather than Roger. He had a pension fund at
SAIS worth a few hundred thousand dollars, and the beneficiary turned out to be Carol Austin, who had at one
point been identified on a form as Denny's fiancée but
hadn't seen Denny in years except for some chance meetings on the street, and had been married to somebody else
for a decade. I was surprised at first, and then it occurred
to me that she had, in fact, been the person Denny had
been closest to as an adult; if she had been removed as
beneficiary, who was there to put in her place? The main
part of the estate consisted of the house in Georgetown—
which was fully paid off and, given the neighborhood,
worth a good deal of money—and some stocks and bonds.
The total turned out to be more than three-quarters of a
million dollars. According to the will Tersh had done for

Denny, it was to be divided in two. The interest from one half was to be used to support Denny's mother if it turned out that she was still alive. At her death, the principal would revert to the beneficiary of the other half—Yale University.

26

I suppose Scott Thompson was right when he said that Denny had been "depressed all of his life." It appears that Denny was depressed, at least at times, even during those shining moments that Peter Krogh and Pudge Henkel conjured up at the memorial service. It's possible to see his life as a steadily less successful attempt to mask that depression. An argument could be made, I'm sure, that what should surprise us about Denny is not that he came to that end but that he managed that beginning. Denny's mother was, in the words of someone who knew her, "depressed for years"; if his state of mind was at least partly genetic, maybe he would have been deeply depressed in his fifties even if he had settled for a life of modest ambition in San Carlos, California. If so, maybe his problems had nothing to do with "honors, expectations, and nonfulfillment" or with a doomed attempt to fit into the "poisonous template of the fifties"—but I know that not many people who knew Denny when the sun shone on him so brilliantly would ever believe that. The quotation that Denny's life and death brought to Diana Thomson's mind, she told me, was from

Cyril Connolly: "Whom the gods wish to destroy they first call promising."

Did we make up a life for Denny to lead? We may have, although he was, at least for a time, a partner in that enterprise. There are times when I think that those of us who were close to him made up, or at least exaggerated, the proportions of his promise: at our thirty-fifth reunion, which happened to take place just after I had spent months thinking about Denny, I was startled to encounter some people who couldn't quite place him. When I told a novelist I know about Denny, he said, "Maybe you all just needed a hero, so you could lead ordinary lives." Nearly the same words were used by a man I spoke to in Washington—an obviously sensible and educated young man I'll call Ned —who had known Denny and who had briefly had a relationship with him. Ned told me that he had taken Denny home to dinner once—Ned's parents, who lived near Washington, were aware of their son's sexual orientation —and that his father had taken him aside after the meal to advise that he not get involved with Denny. Phrases like "inappropriately intense" were used.

"Denny used to wow everyone's parents," I said.

Ned obviously found that hard to believe. He tried not to be impolitely incredulous as I told him about Denny at Yale—like a lot of people who knew Roger D. Hansen in Washington, he couldn't remember whether he had known that Roger had gone to Yale, and was certainly unaware that anything heroic had happened to him there—but he seemed to have a lot of trouble accepting the possibility that the person I described could have been the person he knew. "Maybe you just needed a hero," Ned said.

Our expectations for Denny were heroic, but they were, of course, expectations based on a rigid fifties notion of success that was, as Pudge had observed at the memorial service, "silly and presumptuous." I know now that if my father had been alive to make his regular inquiries about Denny—and if I had managed to remain in Denny's life —I could have reported some accomplishments that represented success in my father's eyes. Denny did some fine work. More than that, what Robert Tucker had described as Denny's "fierce defense of principles of right conduct" was something that my father considered more important than fine work. What Denny's colleagues saw as scrupulosity is not far from my father's way of judging people; when I don't consciously temper that voice from Kansas City, it's not that far from my own way of judging people. Roger Hansen wasn't much like Denny, but I found a lot about him to admire. I think he was worthwhile. I think my father would have felt the same way, even though he would surely have regretted the fact that Denny failed to use that million-dollar smile for so long that it eventually faded away.

A lot of the people I talked to about Denny seemed to be continuing the analysis of the people in the "Big Chill" session who tried to figure out why he had taken his own life. Some of them asked me if he had AIDS, and I sometimes answered, "He didn't need AIDS." I don't know what he had, but I know what he didn't have: his health, his work, somebody to share his life with. For those of us who define our lives in terms of our families, he was unimaginably alone. And he didn't have that sense of worth that translates into capital to draw on in hard times—those moments when you have to make some adaptation to life. I don't know where that sense comes from, but I suspect part of it is reflected in a phrase Robert Keohane used in talking about what Denny lacked: "this kind of underlying self-confidence that whatever he's doing must be right because his parents taught him when he was two that it was." Looking into Denny's life made me realize that what my father had given me was not an even start with the sons of industrialists but something that a lot of parents manage to give their children without concocting a Grand Plan: the security that comes from knowing for sure that they believe you to be a special case.

Still, I don't know why Denny killed himself. After all these years of poking around in other people's lives, I'm convinced that we can almost never know the precise motives of someone else, even old friends. The one person among Denny's friends who resented my inquiry into Denny's life—the young man who had briefly lived with him in Washington—seemed offended when I referred to Denny as an old friend.

"Roger would have said that you didn't know him at all," he told me.

"I couldn't agree with you more," I said.